MODEL BREAKERS

MODEL BREAKERS

Breaking through Stereotypes and Embracing Your Authenticity

Charlene Wang

NEW DEGREE PRESS

MODEL BREAKERS

Breaking through Stereotypes and Embracing Your Authenticity

ISBN

978-1-63676-956-1 *Paperback*

978-1-63730-022-0 *Kindle Ebook*

978-1-63730-124-1 *Digital Ebook*

To my lovely husband Chris,
with whom I create this beautiful life

To my amazing parents, for inspiring me to serve
the world and chase my wildest dream

CONTENTS

AUTHOR'S NOTE

When I first decided to write this book, I thought it would be a collection of family letters to my younger brother Warren.

Warren and I weren't close. It wasn't until he reached out for college advice that I realized how little we knew about each other. We had shared a house for sixteen years, but I couldn't remember the last time we had a genuine conversation. It all seemed kind of silly. How did I not know the name of his favorite Netflix show, his favorite food, or his aspiring dreams?

Warren was surprised when I asked about his life, but he slowly opened up to share his deep dreams and fears with me. After years of assuming I knew my brother well, I realized I had no idea who he was.

I knew Warren was brilliant, but I had no idea how he thought about the world. I wanted to learn more about Warren and share my private struggles in America. I wrote about the journey to find a legal job and to find my voice.

As I shared these letters online, I began to hear back from Warren and hundreds of people on the internet. I realized these topics are more significant than our family exchanges. The letters quickly grew into a book for you, the people who have struggled to find their voice and embrace their authentic self.

This book is about becoming who you want to be.

INTRODUCTION

The moment I heard comedian Ali Wong talk about letting a homeless person into her body or about peeing all over her husband's hands, I knew Wong was going to spark a movement.[1] The world has never seen someone like Ali Wong push the boundaries of class and race by headlining sexual material. Chinese American culture has never had someone like Ali Wong powerfully violate the cultural code and embrace her identity in the most vulnerable moments on stage.

Ali Wong is a Chinese-Vietnamese American comedian who headlines her heritage and identity in stand-up comedy. Instead of playing safe or telling delightful stories, Wong reveals personal anecdotes that most people would be too ashamed to bring up to their best friends. Wong subverts those conventions with her outlandish physical comedy on stage and deliriously detailed sexual matters in her jokes. She outright denies the shame she was raised with. By fully embracing her authentic self, Wong turns shame into power

1 *Ali Wong: Baby Cobra*, directed by Jay Karas, written by Ali Wong, featuring Ali Wong, aired May 5, 2016 on Netflix.

and makes the audience love her even more. In turn, she inspires her audience to embrace the real and not-so-pretty parts of their own lives.

Even though she was raised in a culture where Asian women are not supposed to talk about their bodies, the conventions did not limit her from addressing shame and sexuality. Wong instills the same Asian pride in her daughters through her book *Dear Girls*. She challenges her daughters to question the belief that the "model minority" is the golden standard of Asian expectations. While the qualities of the "model minority" might seem like wonderful traits, they do not and should not define an entire race of individuals with distinct personalities and passions. She wants her girls to be proud of their heritage without giving into the model minority stereotype of being quiet, hardworking, and smart. "I have an unusual amount of Asian pride," she writes to them. "I don't want you to grow up wishing you were white…."[2]

1.

In America, the dominant culture views Asian Americans as a "model minority"—a high-achieving racial minority group upon which other minority groups *should* model their behavior. Asian Americans are expected to be humble and diligent. They are also expected to excel in technical fields and acquire advanced degrees. However, this expectation perpetuates a stereotype that limits and inhibits many Asian

---

2 Ali Wong, *Dear Girls: Intimate Tales, Untold Secrets & Advice for Living Your Best Life* (New York: Penguin Press, 2016), p. 137, Kindle.

Americans from recognizing their true potential and pursuing other vocations and avocations.

While it is okay to uphold the stereotype if it feels comfortable and authentic to one's heart, Wong's perspective is imperative to an ever-changing world. What I love about Wong is that she has shattered the model and inspired so many others to break up with the stereotype. I wanted to see if she was unique or part of a larger trend of others working to break that stereotype. What I have learned excites me about the future of being Chinese in America.

Every year, the model minority stereotype is projected upon millions of Chinese in America. With millions affected by this stereotype, it's no wonder that when I first shared my story of writing this book on LinkedIn, thirty private messages from strangers flooded my inbox in the first twenty-four hours.

As I researched the book, I interviewed a few Chinese immigrants who had come to the States for family, education, or work. Story after story, I noticed how the people I interviewed had the same experience: "We keep our heads down and stay very quiet," the *New York Times* editor Laura Kim wrote.[3] We constantly feel that we are not enough. It is the familial and societal pressure to achieve the success of model minorities that drives this feeling of inadequacy. This has made Chinese immigrants feel they are less than their peers, suffer from mental health issues, and give away their potential to live their dreams.

---

3 Laura Kim, ed., "Confronting Asian-American Stereotypes," The New York Times, June 23, 2018.

I first heard of the term "model minority" during a college class on American culture and politics. The professor showed us a *Time Magazine* featuring six young Asian kids on the cover titled "The Asian-American Whiz Kids."[4] *What a great cultural shorthand*, I thought to myself. *We are perceived to be hard-working and smart before we do any actual work. It must be great to have this privilege.* I was happy with this label, not knowing that "model minority" is just another stereotype that makes us feel like we are never enough. As this stereotype blends all of us into one broad stroke, it robs us of our uniqueness.

This stereotype is seeded in our childhood. Growing up, we become familiar with the high expectations society sets for us. At home, we have to achieve more to make our family proud. At school, we have to work hard to be good at math and science. At the workplace, we have to climb the ladder and become the middle manager who is too busy to ask for more. We think that through sheer hard work, we can eventually be successful in this land of opportunity. We get financial security and work our way up through marriage and life. We constantly work to be better, to model the best behavior, and to strive for successes set by social and political systems.

However, we will never be free within these systems that define us so rigidly.

We need to break out of the stereotype to fully become ourselves.

---

4 Ted Thai, "TIME Magazine Cover: Asian-American Whiz Kids," Time Inc, August 31, 1987.

2.

As I began to write and interview the story of other first- and second-generation Chinese immigrants, I realized that I had repressed a piece of memory for many years.

During my first year at Brown, I built an online education platform that helped Brazilian students find jobs. When I saw a generous alumnus offering office hours through the entrepreneurship center, I got excited about the prospect of showing him this side project. He had a successful career in startup investing, and I was eager to learn from him to benefit my project. *This is going to be a perfect match*, I thought to myself.

While I was waiting for my turn, I overheard a conversation between the alumnus and another student mentee. Just like me, he was young and inexperienced. Just like me, he was interested in venture capital but didn't know where to start. Compelled by his enthusiasm, the alumni mentor shared a series of financial modeling training he put together for a program. They clearly bonded, and the generosity of the alumni mentor impressed me.

When it was my turn, I went in, greeted the mentor, and told him about my project. When I shared the problem I was facing, he cut my elevator pitch short. The alumnus didn't look excited at all. Instead of letting me finish the sentence, he frowned and looked at his phone. He made me feel like I was wasting his time. Then he looked back into my eyes, put on a deeper tone, and advised, "It's hard to help someone who doesn't speak good English. You should learn to speak first. Then you can worry about startup strategy."

The brutal feedback made me pause and wonder whether I was speaking to the same person who had been so supportive of the other student. At that time, I stuttered and blushed, further proving his point that my English was not deserving of his attention.

That fifteen-minute shaming hit me hard. I remained silent and lost the confidence to speak up for myself. I didn't know how to call out his bias. Instead of speaking up and pointing out his ignorance, I let the stereotype of being quiet and accepting define me.

I lost the confidence to pitch to any other investors for the next six months. I questioned myself and overlooked my unique set of entrepreneurial skills. Whenever we had to pitch, I retreated and let my cofounder do the talking, adding a few notes if needed. I never brought up this issue to anyone, not even my cofounder. Only after many pitches and years did I realize that I wasn't the one who needed to be sorry.

A few years later, I still felt passionate about venture capital. When another opportunity arose, however, I refused to remain silent.

When questioned by another angel investor about whether I was qualified, I showed him my track record and the unique career experiences few people had at my age.

I knew who I was. I knew my voice was powerful.

Therefore, I took complete control, pushed back his stereotypes, and proved myself. My self-awareness changed his perceptions. My conviction gave me the power to tell the story on my own terms. It is so rare that we have a chance to change the stories and amend our memories of being quieted in the past.

3.

This story of silencing and stereotyping is not unique to me. And neither should be the story of breaking away from the stereotype and speaking up. After talking to a few friends, I was impressed by the unique personal story shared among Chinese immigrants. We risked invalidating all our past accomplishments to start from scratch without much guidance.

However, we rarely know, let alone celebrate, how far we have come. With this book, I hope to shatter the model minority stereotype and show why our *individual* stories and histories matter.

Instead of the model minority, we are model breakers. As model breakers, we move beyond the Chinese immigrant and Chinese American stereotypes, powerfully own who we are, and realize our full potential.

While the model minority stereotype has affected and limited many Asians, I cannot speak to other Asians' experiences because we live very different lives. I'm breaking away from the generalized model minority stereotype that groups all Asian cultures into a single category. I am solely speaking for the Chinese experience. This is a book for Chinese immigrants who took the risk to come to start a new chapter in America, Chinese Americans who don't see themselves as Chinese but don't feel American enough, and all curious citizens who want to learn more about their Chinese friends.

No matter which group you belong to, you're here because you care about the story that is often hidden from data and headlines. In this book, you will learn about how the lack of self-awareness made Chinese Americans vulnerable and how the lack of community made us victims of the model minority stereotype. You will learn how to challenge the beliefs that kept us quiet, appeal the rules that limited our dreams, and turn limiting stereotypes into powerful narratives.

Model Breakers is a work of nonfiction that speaks to people like my brother Warren; all the first-, second-, and third-generation Chinese Americans; and allies who want to create empowering identities for themselves.

PART 1

CHAPTER 1

HISTORY OF CHINESE AS MODEL MINORITY

Dear Warren,

If you could rewrite the history, what would you like to tell the world?

1.

The model minority stereotype minimizes who we are.

When we were nobody, we could quietly hide under the invisibility cloak and work hard. When we are no longer invisible, the invisibility cloak that helped us in the past might come after us. This stereotype not only made us externalize our success but also internalize our failures.

As poet Prageeta Sharma wrote in "A Situation for Mrs. Biswas," the model minority image initially shielded

Sharma's father. As a visiting professor moonlighting as a security guard at the Museum of Fine Arts, he exemplified the hard work and intelligence central to the stereotype. However, when he became the first South Asian president of a college, he was no longer invisible. Colleagues ridiculed and minimized his success, shaming him as a "greedy brown man, a con, a snake-oil man."[5] The model minority image that initially shielded Sharma's father backfired. He was no longer the good, invisible minority who gave and never asked for anything in return.

The model minority stereotype wipes us out of the grand American narrative.

The idea of Chinese Americans as the "model minority" is rooted early in American history. It was enforced by immigration policy and perpetuated by cultural and economic forces. Though it might seem that Chinese Americans have thrived in America, we have mostly been excluded.

The twentieth and twenty-first centuries have given us beautiful hits like *The Joy Luck Club* and *Crazy Rich Asians* that bring positive Chinese culture representations to attention. Most of the time, Chinese narratives are forgotten or demonized, leading to rising hatred toward Chinese across the society, phrases like "Chinese virus," which fuels xenophobia and even street violence.[6]

---

5 Prageeta Sharma, "A Situation for Mrs. Biswas," Academy of American Poets, 2010.

6 Katie Rogers, Lara Jakes, and Ana Swanson, "Trump Defends Using 'Chinese Virus' Label, Ignoring Growing Criticism," *The New York Times*, March 18, 2020.

The anti-Chinese sentiment is nothing new. It has been rooted in American history for centuries.

In 1862, the US Congress passed the Anti-Coolie Act to appease white people who were nervous that Chinese people were taking away opportunities during the California Gold Rush. The government taxed hard-working Chinese businesspeople to calm angry, insecure white voters.[7]

In 1869, 15,000 Chinese people built the 700-mile transcontinental railroad from Sacramento, California to Promontory, Utah. These Chinese workers lived in tents and were paid less than their American counterparts.[8]

In 1880, white people's economic anxiety led to Denver's anti-Chinese Riot. Thousands of white men mobbed, burned, and killed Chinese men without any penalty.[9]

In 1882, the US government introduced the Chinese Exclusion Act, the first and only immigration law to prevent all Chinese folks from immigrating to the States, a country built by immigrants.[10]

In 1965, President Lyndon B. Johnson lifted the immigration ban, but only highly educated and skilled Asian

---

7 "Thirty-Seventh Congress, Sess. II, Ch. 25, 27 1862," accessed January 4, 2021.

8 Nadja Sayej, "'Forgotten by Society' – How Chinese MIGRANTS Built the Transcontinental Railroad," July 18, 2019.

9 Mark R. Ellis, "Denver's Anti-Chinese Riot," Encyclopedia of the Great Plains, accessed January 4, 2021.

10 History.com Staff, "Chinese Exclusion Act," HISTORY, A&E Television Networks, August 24, 2018.

professionals—doctors, engineers, and mechanics—were granted visas.[11]

Since 1965, when US immigration policy only allowed highly skilled Asians to enter the country, the model minority stereotype took shape. These well-educated, hard-working, dedicated over-achievers became the model for all Asian Americans. Soon popularized by political propaganda during the Cold War, the US government came up with the idealized model all minorities had to adhere to or risk exclusion. "American policymakers became really attentive to putting their best image out into the world and winning hearts and minds in Asia," Ellen Wu, author of *The Color of Success*, said in an interview with the *Washington Post*.[12] This political propaganda assured Asian Americans that as long as they worked hard, they would overcome discrimination and be allowed to achieve their American Dreams.

The promise turned out to be a false one.

Poet Cathy Park Hong wrote about her Asian American experiences in *Minor Feelings*. In the book, Hong discusses the theory of minor feelings, the cognitive dissonance toward the model minority myth. Such sentiments are ingrained in the structural inequity to make us feel less than. Based on her personal experiences, Hong said, "**We will not be the power but become absorbed by power**, not share the power of whites but be stooges to a white ideology that exploited our ancestors."[13]

---

11 "Model Minority Section," Stereotypes, Identity, and Belonging Lab (SIBL) at the University of Washington, 2011.

12 Jeff Guo, "The Real Reasons the US Became Less Racist toward Asian Americans," *The Washington Post*, April 29, 2019.

13 Cathy Park Hong, *Minor Feelings: An Asian American Reckoning* (New York: One World, 2020), p. 34, Kindle.

Over time, this model minority myth makes us forget we are uniquely beautiful.

2.

Maybe that is why my cousin Amelia found her childhood to be so confusing. Growing up in a predominantly white neighborhood in Westwood, Massachusetts, Amelia hated being Asian for the first nine years of her life. While she received an excellent education in a wealthy community, she struggled to find people who looked like her. The diversity was so bad that the school district even developed a program to bus students from Boston to diversify the school.

Amelia struggled with her identity early on. "My childhood was so confusing that I didn't know who I was," she confessed. She looked different from all the other white kids in her class. She ate pork and rice while others ate Caesar salad or mac and cheese. Being so different was quite scary to a five year old.

Amelia was similar to Honey Nut Cheerios:

Like Honey Nut Cheerios
A Little Small,
Lightly Golden,
And Surrounded By White

— APRI PARK, HONEY NUT CHEERIOS[14]

---

14 *Apri Park*, "'Honey Nut Cheerios' - a Poem about Growing up Asian-American," April 8, 2019, video, 2:55.

All she wanted was to fit in and not underscore the differences between herself and her classmates.

Amelia quit the Sunday Chinese School in an attempt to fit in. Even though she is ethnically Chinese, she only wanted to speak English. She never felt a strong connection to her Chinese heritage, besides enjoying dim sum. Growing up at a predominantly white school, the kids at her neighborhood school called her *Whasian*, a racial slur calling out to her as a white person trapped inside a Chinese body. And since she only studied American history at school, she questioned her heritage and wondered whether people like her had their own history at all.

This cultural shaming stuck with her until she transferred to a private school with better education and diversity. In her new class, there was only one white kid. Surrounded by Asian Americans from Quincy, Massachusetts, and African Americans from Jamaica Plain, Massachusetts, Amelia finally saw that she was not that different. "I really started to find myself and realize that I shouldn't be ashamed of my culture," she told me. "I need to be proud of who I am."

To get back in touch with her own culture, she even tried to live up to the Asian stereotypes of being quiet, working hard, and getting straight As. Yet even when she tried her best, it was tough to live up to expectations created only to limit us. She didn't know the history of the model minority, and she didn't see a world where Chinese people were proud of being themselves. She lost herself while searching for external validation.

Despite Amelia's love for her new school, she felt she had betrayed her own culture for the first nine years of life. She wanted to get in touch with her Chinese heritage so she could connect with her family, but she was too afraid to share these struggles with her parents.

3.

When I first came to America for a summer camp at Phillips Academy in Andover, Massachusetts, I had many plans. I wanted to become more fluent in English and create a future of more growth and wonder. However, I had a hard time connecting with people in social settings. I wanted to talk like Americans and cover up my spotty accents. I ended up speeding up my speech, hoping that no one could catch the grammatical errors in between. I later learned that English is a slow language from my public speaking professor Barbara Tannenbaum.

My speedy speech often brought more confusion and attention. Sometimes, I struggled to tell my classmates how much I wanted to be their friends. Sometimes, I raised my hands halfway and shivered at the thought that I might not have enough vocabulary to express myself. If only I could speak like a native, I believed people would be able to understand what I wanted to say.

Each of these experiences left me very self-conscious. I had so much more to say, but I was too busy rehearsing those syllables in my head. Plus, I was worried that everyone would find out how different (weird) I was.

I ended up remaining silent inside and outside of classes. I also started playing introvert in life; hoping the quiet badge would shield my weaknesses. This language barrier distanced me from Amelia and my full self.

When I came back to America for college, I tried to skip most orientation activities and stayed in my dorm. When my friends invited me to freshman social events, I would come up with excuses. The computer lab became my hideout spot when my roommate threw parties in our tiny dorm room. I strived for more connections, but I was stuck with more social anxiety until I met other shy friends in my sophomore year.

While people call my alumni Brown University "the party Ivy," I graduated without attending a single party. My shyness came from being confined within the model minority stereotype. By hiding the joyful and social part of myself, I contributed to the silence because it was all I knew at the time.

Language barrier. Social anxiety. Model Minority. These forces silence us.

4.

We live under a veil of ignorance that whispers, *If you put your heads down and accumulate more wealth, people will see you as successful.* Growing up, many immigrant parents would advise their kids to stay in their lane, which is the exact opposite of the outspoken and bold American culture.[15]

---

15 I was really grateful for the unique way my parents raised me. They love me unconditionally and want me to be myself.

This cultural difference may explain why the Chinese American voting demographic had one of the lowest voter turnout rates. While 65 percent of white people and 59 percent of Black people voted, only 41 percent of Chinese people voted in the 2016 United States presidential election.[16] This turnout discrepancy would indicate Chinese Americans don't organize or feel disenfranchised around American politics, which supports the toxic myth that Chinese are "naturally" quiet. Nothing could be further from the truth. We are, after all, talking about the same people who organized the 1989 Tiananmen Square protests—one of the most revolutionary movements in recent history.[17]

American politics and culture have eroded our history of rebellion. When I look for successful Chinese American leaders in society, I cannot help but notice their lack of ethnic traces. In an American-centric world, the system rewards individuals who can adjust to mainstream values and stereotypes. Even though I grew up attending a local school in Taipei, I would intentionally act like an American. I was, and still am now, very conscious of how I speak. In high school, I would force myself to read literature like *The Great Gatsby* and *The Adventures of Huckleberry Finn* to better prepare for the SAT. After attending the unconscious bias training at work, I adopted a deeper tone, spoke slowly, and took up a more expansive stance so that others would subconsciously perceive me as a trustworthy leader. After all, mainstream success often depends on how well we assimilate into society.

---

16 Karthick Ramakrishnan, "The Asian American Vote in 2016: Record Gains, but Also Gaps," Data Bits, May 19, 2017.

17 History.com Editors, "Tiananmen Square Protests," May 31, 2019.

Over the last fifty years, our thoughts have been infiltrated by propaganda that denies our existence. Recent examples, such as Scarlett Johansson's casting in *Ghost in the Shell*, received more vocal backlash. "It reduces race to mere physical appearance as opposed to culture, social experience, identity, history," *Crazy Rich Asians* lead actress Constance Wu tweeted.[18] Despite the public backlash, whitewashing is repeatedly used across Western history, literature, and mass culture, proving that we don't exist. While we cannot go back in time to change the narrative written in place, we can start writing a more empowering history now. If we don't tell our story, **people won't even bother to understand the difference**. If we accept silence and play safe, we are giving in to the racist reality.

While silence, when used strategically, may lead to financial success (we will talk more about this tradeoff in Chapter Ten), this perpetual silence has diminished the success of people like Prageeta Sharma's father and compromised our race's integrity. No matter how hard we work, we still struggle to find our voice and achieve our full potential.

I can't help but notice the silencing trope played in our lives. After I hopped over the language barrier that stood between Amelia and me, I was surprised to learn that just like me, she felt like an extrovert but played introvert to fit in. When I asked her why she couldn't just be herself, she told me she was afraid to let people down. She was scared to disappoint the people who expected her to be someone else. She struggled to be fully herself.

---

18 Melissa Chan, "Photo of Scarlett Johansson in Ghost in the Shell Reignites 'Whitewashing' Controversy," *Time*, April 18, 2016.

I didn't tell her about my story back then because I forgot that I had been through something similar. Now that I bounced back from my early rejections and learned to tell my own story, I have created a playbook to help Amelia—and millions of people like her—rewrite a story that feels more authentic and empowering for their life.

Democracy in America is not a spectator sport. We cannot change the country's history without participation. If we don't fight for our rights, no one will. People will assume that our community doesn't need support. And if we don't fight for other people's rights, no one will fight for us. We need to raise our voices and share our struggles. We need to vote for every policy and for leaders who uphold our values; from school boards, to state attorneys, to the president.

We need to break the model minority stereotype. Some of us are high achievers while others are slackers. Some are lazy. Some are artistic. Some like math while others like literature. Some are outspoken while others are quiet. To paint us all with a single brush, no matter how positive that brush might be, is to deny us who we really are.

We are not the model minority. We are who we are.

CHAPTER 2

REDEFINE THE STEREOTYPES

Dear Warren,

How many times have you looked at a person and thought you know them already?

1.

Stereotypes make up the air we breathe.

We take cognitive shortcuts to make sense of the world. These perceptions, often made quickly and subconsciously, are rooted in how we are raised and behave. They are so ingrained in our minds that we forget they are all made up by ourselves, parents, teachers, or people in power. These stereotypes are so subtle that we've never thought to confront them. They have become such a part of our subconscious that we can hardly feel their existence.

We all have stereotypes. Stereotypes make us associate a person with their demographic traits. Stereotypes fool us into thinking we know someone more than we do. Stereotypes make us judge whether the other group is "good enough" to become a part of us. Stereotypes make us stupid.

We often base these stereotypes on our limited experiences and access to information. It is even more problematic when we allow an inherited stereotype to determine our identity. Since childhood, we Chinese Americans have been taught to strive for perfection. We strive for the perfect grade, the perfect image, and the perfect job. To make our family proud, we attempt to prove ourselves by working twice as hard and being twice as good. However, when someone doesn't know us, they make assumptions and associations, regardless of who we are.

We may want to clean out stereotypes from the air we breathe, but we are getting ahead of ourselves.

People are wired to see the world through stereotypes. As Daniel Kahneman explained in *Thinking, Fast and Slow*, most of our decisions are driven by heuristics and cognitive biases. This lazy thinking saves us energy and defaults our minds to stereotypes.[19] Therefore, we need stereotypes. Our brain relies on stereotypes to deal with the abundant information without exhausting our brain. We want stereotypes to swiftly react to emergencies and take care of daily decisions, such as what to eat for dinner or where to go for vacation.

---

19 Daniel Kahneman, *Thinking, Fast and Slow* (New York: Farrar, Straus and Giroux, 2011).

Stereotypes are essential in daily life, reducing the spontaneous cognition we would otherwise have to perform at every moment. They maximize our efficiency and are incredibly powerful. Their power and subtlety are precisely why we must be aware of our relationship to stereotypes.

2.

We see the world, including ourselves, through stereotypes. The model minority stereotype is driving millions of Asian Americans toward an illusion of success and burnout. I had the same experience too.

Growing up, I was the top student of the class, president of various clubs, recipient of multiple national awards, and many more. Even though my parents put no external pressure on me, I could feel the invisible expectation to carry on their legacy and become a "model student." To accelerate my growth, I would skip multiple grades to take advanced math, English, and coding classes. While I am grateful for all those learning opportunities, I always felt the pressure to work harder being the youngest person in the room. Whenever I doubted why I was in the room, my mother would tell me, "You will learn the most if you are the least competent person in the room." Or, to put it more bluntly, "What doesn't kill you makes you stronger."

However, the obsession with being a top student took a toll on my health. In December 2018, a few weeks after I handed in my final papers, I began to experience acute pain from my nervous system.

The moment I landed at the Taiwan Taoyuan International Airport, I experienced pain. It felt almost like someone was thrusting a sharp needle into my head repeatedly. My entire body spiked with discomfort. I could hardly walk or carry my luggage, let alone stand. Tension and discomfort rumbled through my body as I tried to explain to make sense of what was wrong with me; my face and lips felt like they were on fire. I blamed the pain on the sudden change of atmosphere and the hot, humid air. Thinking that pain would go away soon, I pushed myself through customs and hopped on a ride home.

When I finally returned home, I took a quick shower and described the symptoms to my mom. There were no apparent wounds, but the pain was buzzing from my facial nerve. Drinking water felt like swallowing fire. Even the wind on the road felt like a knife cutting through my face.

My mom and her doctor friends diagnosed my symptom as trigeminal neuralgia (TN), a neurological symptom that sent electric shocks across my face. Research shows that twelve out of every 100,000 people get TN every year, and it is most common in people older than fifty.[20] It was so rare to see TN in a twenty-something. No one in my family circle knew how or why this was happening. My doctors could not suggest anything besides a bag of painkillers. Yet, I knew what was going on and suspected that painkillers were the furthest thing from the solution.

---

20 Staff Writer, "Five Things You Should Know about Trigeminal Neuralgia," MHealth.org, July 27, 2016.

Since I came to the States, I was always chasing one goal after another. I always had something to work on, whether side projects, internships, or research. I often worked late nights and during holidays. In 2018, I finally got everything I wanted: a cool research project, a shiny internship, and a wonderful partner. That was the first time in three years when I finally went on a break.

When the break started, my hyper-stressed nervous system finally got to breathe. Then it broke down.

The TN was just the tip of the iceberg.

3.

I was stuck in the box.

I couldn't find a trace of TN when I looked back on my calendar and journals. I saw the calendar filled with golf lessons and social chats, acting as if my pain never happened. Subconsciously, I refused to believe or even admit that a chronic pain was growing inside me. I tried to heal myself by getting busy and repressed my feelings until I had no energy left.

Only when I fully accepted that I had chronic pain with stress did I begin to see a way out. I forced myself to do nothing for the next two weeks. Some days, I would receive physical therapy and Chinese medicine to calm my vagus nerve, giving space for my neurons to breathe. Some nights, I woke up on a soaked pillow, dreading that I could never have a "normal" face again.

Once I realized how naïve it was to ignore the critical body signals, I adopted deep rest and mindfulness practice.

While the pain lasted for three weeks, TN changed how I lived my life.

4.

I began to revisit my perception of myself. Instead of seeing myself as a high-achieving person who can secure all the fancy titles, I focused on my potential to learn and grow. I studied neuroscience and psychology to learn more about my mind and stumbled upon the growth mindset.

Carol S. Dweck is the leading researcher in motivation and the author of *Mindset*. The growth mindset, according to Dweck, is "based on the belief that your basic qualities are things you can cultivate through your efforts, your strategies, and help from others." On the other hand, the fixed mindset is based on the belief that "your qualities are carved in stone." When confronted with the model minority stereotype, people with the growth mindset are more likely to distance themselves from this label.

Growth mindset is a spectrum. We often display a fixed mindset toward our weaknesses and a growth mindset toward strengths. Dweck found that negative labels and stereotypes can be especially damaging to people who showed fixed mindsets. When confronted with negative stereotypes, people with growth mindsets are much more likely to see the label as blatantly wrong and vigorously prove them wrong. As we bring more awareness toward how our lives have been affected by the fixed mindset, we can replace the excuses and self-blame with courage and agency. There may be resistance at the beginning of this break-up with the old part of ourselves, just like many break-ups. Therefore, we need to remind ourselves that this break-up is to leave the mindset that no longer serves us and embrace the possibility of a beautiful, courageous future.

5.

The breakdown in my health was ultimately a gift. It forced me to confront the stereotypes I had imposed upon myself and redefine the stereotypes others had for me.

If I could go back to the moment when the alumni mentor rejected me, I would acknowledge his stereotypes said nothing about me. The stereotype merely reflected his personal experience. Perhaps, I reminded him of a foreign language he had struggled to learn or a foreign founder he had struggled to connect with. Either way, his personal reaction would not change the fact that many immigrants are amazing founders.

Once I understood that his stereotype simply reflected his own struggle, I could revisit his action with compassion. Although he hurt my confidence, he also triggered me to learn more about how stereotypes could affect our lives. After all, we are all imperfect humans. We take cognitive shortcuts and try our best to connect with each other.

Since stereotypes would not go away, I could choose to face it directly. With that new perception, I would approach his behavior with curiosity and say, "Thank you for being candid. You seem to be knowledgeable but frustrated. What goals would you like to achieve with mentoring?" By acknowledging his action and reaction, I can shift from reacting negatively to creating a better future together.

When used wisely, stereotypes are our friends.

Harvard Business School professor Laura Huang provides a framework to redefine the stereotypes in her book *Edge*. She wrote, "You can accept the perceptions of others so that you can consciously address them and confront them—but without embracing and internalizing them. The views of others are overwhelmingly not about you at all—they're about their insecurities, their own goals, and their attempts to reconcile their sense of self-awareness."[21] Once you know that the perceptions of others have little to do with who you are, you may defuse the frustrations by slowing down for a moment and asking a few curious questions, such as:

1. What implicit assumptions might come up in their head?
2. What experiences may have influenced their assumptions?
3. How would their assumptions affect their actions?
4. What end goal are they trying to achieve with their actions?

This pause gives us time to understand their point of view and empathize with their feelings. **When we are open to feeling their emotions, we will find our shared similarities and better connect as humans.** With this new awareness, we can

---

21 Laura Huang, *Edge: Turning Adversity Into Advantage* (New York: Penguin, 2020).

replace their old story with the unique values we bring to the table. You may also go to the exercise at the end of Chapter Six to get you started.

6.

When I started my coaching service at twenty-two, many people questioned, "What can someone at such a young age offer to someone with decades of career experience?" The implicit assumption is that coaching requires wisdom that can only be acquired through aging. When I met prospective clients, I would proactively address their sentiments and share success stories that speak to their backgrounds and interests. To effectively address their skepticism, I would offer a powerful exercise that helps them tap into their intuition, identify their key values, and make better decisions—all in twenty minutes. By meeting them where they were and overturning their stereotypes, I could redefine their perceptions and coach hundreds of entrepreneurs in one year. As Kevin Lee, cofounder of the healthy ramen brand immi, said, "I've spoken with a few coaches in my lifetime, but you are on a whole other level."

As Professor Huang said to me in a Zoom call, "Once you know your underestimated strengths and weaknesses, you may say something that makes people pause for a second and see you in a slightly different light. That's how you get that new opportunity to have a deeper and richer conversation with them." By redefining their perceptions, I was able to create new opportunities for myself to shine. When I take the power back and celebrate my unique voice, I can truly be who I am.

7.

Once we show society how different we are from the stereotypes, the stereotypes can no longer hold us back. All it takes is the courage to speak up and step into powerful opportunities in our lives.

In this chapter, we studied how to redefine stereotypes and bring awareness to our community and ourselves. In the next few chapters, we will dive into steps to embrace who we are and tell our own story. We need to know that no labels can define us. With self-awareness, we can rewrite our narratives, build support networks, and build our risk appetite to empower ourselves. It is okay to feel uncomfortable or emotional.

While stereotypes are often pervasive and harmful, we have the power to redefine the stereotypes in our favor.

CHAPTER 3

WHY IS IT IMPORTANT TO BREAK THE MODEL NOW?

Dear Warren,

You told me that you were waiting for the right time to speak up, yet there is no better time than now.

1.

In April 2017, a Vietnamese American doctor named David Dao boarded the United Express Flight 3411, leaving Chicago and heading home to Elizabethtown, Kentucky. He was about to open a free clinic for veterans, having graduated from medical school in Saigon in 1974 and immigrated to the US a year later as a Vietnamese refugee. He then was forced to enroll in another medical school to regain his medical license. He built his practice in Kentucky and realized his American Dream.[22]

Dr. Dao was one of the four passengers selected to get off the overbooked United Express Flight 3411 and make room for their airline employees. Right after Dr. Dao was selected to leave the plane, he patiently called United Airlines. He pleaded to stay because he needed to see patients the next day. Then, the security guard pressed him to get off the plane or go to jail. Dr. Dao was polite and articulated that he had to stay. Moments later, he was seized, dragged, and yanked off the plane. He was screaming to go home while blood ran over his face.[23] He managed to re-board the plane once, grasping onto the final string of the American Dream that brought him to the US four decades ago. He, once again, collapsed into unconsciousness in the face of a laughing security guard.[24]

This interaction, recorded on many cellphone cameras from all angles, has been viewed several million times on YouTube. It even made international headlines.[25]

Dr. Dao suffered a severe concussion, a broken nose, and two missing teeth.

---

22 David Dao, *Dragged Off: Refusing to Give Up My Seat on the Way to the American Dream* (Florida: Mango, 2021), Kindle.

23 Daniel Victor and Matt Stevens, "United Airlines Passenger Is Dragged From an Overbooked Flight," *The New York Times*, April 10, 2017.

24 Jason Powell, "I Was on United Flight 3411. Here's What I Saw.," Chicago Tribune, May 10, 2019.

25 *Inside Edition*, "Doctor Was On Phone With United Moments Before Being Dragged Off Plane," April 12, 2017, video, 2:49.

In April 2019, Dao reflected on the incident and said that he did not remember being taken off the plane. When he watched the footage, he "just cried."[26] When he saw his daughter Crystal Dao speaking up for him, he wrapped his arms around and, again, "just cried." Dao was not expecting such violence. He was trying to see patients in his hometown.

"The accident turned out the positive way," Dao told ABC News. "The airline business has changed the policy. I'm not angry with them. They have a job to do. If they don't do it, they may lose their job."[27] Even after that inhumane treatment, Dao still believes in humans. Since his retirement, he is dedicating his time to philanthropy.

Dao was dehumanized. What happened to Dao could have happened to any one of our dads.

If we do not speak up for our community, who will?

2.

The David Dao case was not a unique event in American public life.

Every year, the model minority stereotype is projected upon millions of Chinese in America. You will read about Candice who left her only family in America to start a new chapter in

26 *ABC News*, "Doctor dragged off United Airlines flight says he 'cried' watching the video," April 9, 2019. video, 4:04.

27 Ibid.

California, about Irene who struggled to reconcile the culture of her upbringing with the perceptions associated with her ethnicity, and about Janice who carried an invisible wound for twelve years of her life. In these cases, you will learn about how they navigate the external labels and embrace who they truly are.

Chinese immigrants are defined as those who came to the States for family, education, or work. The "immigration" here doesn't necessarily mean having a certain visa status. As long as you have the intent that you could call America home one day, you are an immigrant. While we immigrants grow up learning Chinese history and Confucius' values, we are also familiar with *Friends, CNN*, and the *New York Times.* In addition to buying into the rosy picture of America, our minds are seeded hoping that one day, we could carry out our American Dream.

Little did we know that opportunity in this land is not equal. As much as we hoped to uphold the belief that all men are created equal, we realized that everyone starts with a different baseline. In our home country, we were used to people who looked like us, ate the same food, and shared the same values. We created bubbles around us in which everything is familiar, and nothing challenged who we are or what we believe.

This little bubble is going to burst.

3.

When I first came to the States, I signed up for a few pre-orientation activities before my first semester in college. I attended a program designed to promote interracial understanding.

Throughout the orientation, I met students from Argentina to Nigeria, found my pronouns, and became aware of multiple shades of skin color. Before that orientation, I had never thought about my identity. It shocked me as I learned the history of injustice and colonialism. I learned the vocabulary to describe how each -ism affects lives.

However, I had a tough time seeing myself as part of this diversity and inclusion narrative. I wasn't sure whether I was a minority because they never mentioned my ethnicity or skin color. What was my skin color anyway? I was not as yellow as the banana. Was I beige? I didn't even know how to describe my skin color. I felt even more marginalized by being Chinese. I was not even a part of the overt race dynamics at play in this country. I was afraid that these questions were too trivial, so I never brought them up with anyone.

I wondered whether I am the only one who struggled to find myself in the United States, so I reached out to a few other Chinese international students. I found that many feel betrayed by the promise of the American Dream. "The land of opportunity is not so equal," my college friend Murong Xu said. "There are much fewer opportunities now." I wondered whether Murong would share any bit of my confusion, so I asked her how she saw herself. Surprisingly, despite growing up in Beijing, she told me that she didn't see herself as fully Chinese. Perhaps American education had changed her, yet I soon realized that she didn't identify with Americans either. Her sentiment is not alone. I saw this identity crisis in myself and many of my friends too.

We can trace Murong's fear back to social stereotypes. While Murong honored her traditional Chinese values, she was afraid that being Chinese might limit her growth in American society. Research has shown that even though we have checked all the boxes—Ivy League degree, competitive internships, stellar work performance—we are perceived to lack confidence and assertive communications, which are deemed important leadership traits.[28] From college to the workplace, we are constantly silenced by the stereotypes that dictated who we should be.

I don't want to be silenced anymore.

4.

These stereotypes—the lack of confidence and assertion—are not unique to the immigrants less familiar with how the culture works. These stereotypes are even more severe to Chinese Americans who grow up learning Western narratives. They knew so much about the great West and so little about their great Chinese cultural heritage. The reality is that many Chinese Americans are socialized to believe that our stories are not important. The first decade of education has been about not being different and just going unnoticed, trying to be as culturally American as possible. Even though the grades are the metric of our early life's successes, these grades do materially nothing to help Chinese Americans acclimate well.

The pandemic exacerbated the everyday microaggressions. A sixteen-year-old boy was physically attacked and sent to

---

28 Anemona Hartocollis, "Harvard Rated Asian-American Applicants Lower on Personality Traits, Suit Says," The New York Times, June 15, 2018.

the emergency room simply because he is Asian American.[29] A nineteen-year-old girl was ridiculed that she "smells like dang coronavirus" on her way to the airport. According to the report from the Stop AAPI Hate Youth Campaign, one in four Asian youths have experienced racist bullying over the past year.[30] This does not account for the youths who didn't report or the youths who saw their friends being bullied and didn't know how to fight back. This lack of cultural awareness made us succumb to the history written to compromise our rights. **After all, if you don't know who you are, how can you tell people you are important?**

We have a lot to be proud of, yet we have freely given our power away for the first eighteen years of life. Western education curriculums diminish Asian history and the dominance of Asia throughout history. If we didn't attend a diverse school, we wouldn't learn about the 4,000-year Chinese legacy until we took a college seminar on Asian American Studies. Chinese voices, contributions, and stories are not highlighted in most of my interviewee's core education. Even in City Politics, one of my favorite classes in college, we only got to glance over the racial demographics in one class. We read a lot about race, but I could not find any single reading on Asian Americans. I had hoped to get a more relevant reading assignment during the immigration week, yet I didn't see anything about Asian Americans. Therefore, I emailed the professor

---

29 Christina Capatides, "Bullies Attack Asian American Teen at School, Accusing Him of Having Coronavirus," CBS News, February 14, 2020.

30 Megan Dela Cruz et al, "They Blamed Me Because I am Asian: Findings from Youth-Reported Incidents of AntiAAPI Hate," accessed January 3, 2021.

to ask for an Asian American reading list that tells a powerful narrative like Ta-Nehisi Coates's *Between the World and Me.*[31]

My professor replied, "Great question and I have some great books for you. I'll have a list for you soon!" I followed up and never heard back. I wasn't sure whether I should keep following up. I eventually stopped begging someone to tell me my own history and went on Amazon to find books on Chinese Americans. The closest one I could find was Claire Chao's family memoir *Remembering Shanghai.*[32] I was quite frustrated at how Chinese Americans are marginalized in American education. *Why isn't our history part of the core curriculum? Why isn't our story more central to everyone's learning?*

5.

In the last eighteen months, we have seen the rise and fall of Asian pride. We celebrated the rise of the Asian presidential candidate Andrew Yang. We struggled over the hate crime ignited by the trend of "Chinese Virus." Here is a snapshot of a few incidents that took place in New York City, the social capital of protests and one of the most liberal cities in the world:

---

31 Ta-Nehisi Coates, *Between the World and Me* (New York: Spiegel & Grau, 2015), Kindle.

32 Claire Chao and Isabel Sun Chao, *Remembering Shanghai: A Memoir of Socialites, Scholars and Scoundrels* (Honolulu: Plum Brook, LLC, 2018), Kindle.

- On February 5, 2020, an Asian woman was cursed and severely hit on her head for wearing a mask in Manhattan.[33]

- On March 12, 2020, an Asian woman was told to not "bring that chink virus here" in a nice office building.[34]

- On March 25, 2020, an Asian man was spat on and yelled at "You fu*king Chinese spreading the coronavirus!" in a Brooklyn subway station.[35]

- On July 27, 2020, an eighty-nine-year-old Asian woman was purposely targeted, slapped, and set on fire by two teenagers on the street in the Brooklyn neighborhood.[36]

- On February 19, 2021, a forty-something Asian man was knocked out and suffered a brain hemorrhage after having a drink in Flushing, Queens.[37]

While the world is watching New York City fighting the pandemic, Asian people have to fight to be seen as human in

---

33 Ewan Palmer, "Asian Woman Allegedly Attacked in New York Subway Station for Wearing Protective Mask," *Newsweek*, February 5, 2020).

34 Elizabeth Ho (@RealElizabethHo), "Yo. So the other day I was in an elevator and I used my elbow to touch a button. Old dude says "oh. Coronavirus?" And I was like "don't have it but trying to be prepared," Twitter, March 12, 2020, 8:21 p.m.

35 Tina Moore and Olivia Bensimon, "Asian Man Spat on in Latest Coronavirus Hate Crime in Brooklyn Station," New York Post, March 25, 2020.

36 Carl Samson, "89-Year-Old Chinese American Woman Set on Fire in NYC," *NextShark*, July 27, 2020.

37 Carl Samson, "Chinese Man's Teeth Knocked Out, Suffers Brain Hemorrhage After Random Attack in NYC," *NextShark*, February 23, 2021.

a world that constantly attacks them for being themselves. However, if we didn't fight for what happened to us, how could we structure a collective voice?

This social conundrum is exactly why we need to break the model now. If we don't speak up for ourselves, no one will.

6.

Pushing against the tide is difficult. We have a lot to learn from how other minorities persevere to change public narratives. Otherwise, our complacency will silence our voices, prolong our sufferings, and erode our political status until there is nothing left to tear upon. We need to pick ourselves up, deal with our problems, and turn the systems in our favor.

We are at the crossroad of racial consciousness where #MeToo, Crazy Rich Asians, and Black Lives Matter have the country's attention. We are at a moment where the civil rights movement has ignited people's consciousness to unlearn biases. We need to act now before the fire dies down.

Through my research and interviews, I found that Chinese Americans who are deeply in touch with their own culture and share their stories, are able to experience life with confidence and pride. This gives me hope that we could be successful, despite the many structural failures to overcome.

We must acknowledge how we feel when we are bullied or see people bullied in school. We can fight back when people call us names. We can each send emails to remind our professors to include our history in the curriculum. We can begin to value our voice and share our stories. We can take pride in what we have gone through and help each other build confidence.

The awareness around ourselves, our heritage, and our feelings are critical to defining who we are in society. The more we see ourselves in the community, the more we know that we are not alone. The more we make it to the mainstream culture, the more we can rewrite the narratives that have oppressed our lives. Collectively, we can proudly wear our Chinese badge while changes are underway.

Now is the time to break the model minority and become who we are.

Speak up now.

PART 2

CHAPTER 4

KNOW YOURSELF

Dear Warren,

You said that you know who you are and have always been fine. Keep this confidence with you and nourish it as you grow up.

1.

It took Janet Chang over a decade to find her voice, but I didn't know that when I first met her. Her passionate final presentation in my college political science seminar left me thinking leadership was in her bones. Her confident public presence belied the scars beneath.

Just like most Chinese immigrants, Janet's parents enforced a strong focus on her education. "Racial diversity was not openly discussed in the '90s," Janet told me. "I could not see my culture in the media or school syllabus." In her elementary school, Janet, like many other Asian kids, got bullied in school and didn't know how to fight back. This lack of cultural awareness, coupled with classmates' derogatory comments, made Janet ashamed of who she was.

In addition to being bullied, Janet suffered verbal and physical abuse by her father. She didn't know who to seek for help. She quietly lived with this trauma until she wanted to kill herself. When she spoke up and told her mother about this excruciating pain, her mother just said, "Don't do this to me."

You might be asking yourself, "What was wrong with her parents? Why didn't they follow up with any help?" It's important to remember that Chinese parents are humans carrying their own wounds. Many of them were raised to believe that emotions, including suicidal thoughts, can be ignored through sheer will. No one has told them otherwise.

For the next twelve years, Janet was forced back into silence. Everyone in her family knew what happened, but no one was willing to talk about it. Janet was left to deal with it herself.

Janet could have killed herself, but her will to endure was stronger than her will to die.

2.

Janet's parents suppressed emotions, in themselves and in their daughter.

Many first-generation Asian immigrants, who escaped to the States in the late twentieth century, were culturally oppressed, cash-strapped, and depressed. All they wanted was to survive in this new world. They adopted modest behaviors to avoid trouble. Being quiet, humble, and silent was a necessity.

The epitome of such suppression, according to Asian dating coach J.T. Tran, is the Asian poker face, a term used to describe "the lack of range when it comes to facial expression." Tran explained this to a roomful of Yale undergraduates over master's tea at Silliman College. As laughter filled the room, Tran describes what would typically happen at a "white party with white friends": the repeated questions of "Dude, are you angry?"[38] Although Tran knows a discussion of Asian poker face cues laughter, it's a double-edged sword. It reveals the racist undertones that many Asians are perceived by American society as emotionless or inscrutable. As Janet Chang observed throughout her life, Asians who don't show emotions are often "seen to be less human."

As author Jed Chun wrote, the Asian community is often impacted by the intergenerational trauma from their immigrant families. These families usually mean well but struggle to communicate their good intentions. When these first-generation immigrants became parents, they intuitively passed down their survival "best practices" to the next generation. These patterns may take the form of "using indirect communication, keeping secrets, maintaining silence, keeping oneself isolated, feeling victimized, and fearing external identifiers."[39]

---

38 *ABCs Of Attraction | JT Tran's Dating Advice & PUA Bootcamps for Asian Men*, "Jerry 'JT' Tran at Yale University about Asian American Dating (Part 9)," July 26, 2011, video, 7:01.

39 Jed Chun, "A Reflection on Asian Intergenerational Trauma," Asian Mental Health Collective, November 1, 2019.

Many immigrant parents had to prioritize their survival before they could care for their children's emotions. Therefore, when the childhood trauma happened, children like Janet didn't have the tools to understand their feelings. Dr. Bessel van der Kolk, the world's leading clinician and researcher on childhood trauma, found that "in response to their trauma, and in coping with the dread that persisted long afterward, these patients had learned to shut down the brain areas that transmit the visceral feelings and emotions that accompany and define terror." However, those brain areas also transmit the entire range of emotions that form our self-awareness. By suppressing those triggers, the patients also gave up the opportunity to feel fully alive.[40] They repressed their feelings to protect themselves, not knowing that the shutdown would distance themselves from the wonder of life and hold their future generations back from prospering.

They, just like their parents, didn't know that denial would prolong the suffering further.

However, if we don't know how we feel, how can we know who we are?

3.

What happened to Janet also happened to my friend Grace Chiang.

Grace was the perfect model minority. She had perfect SAT scores, graduated from Yale University as a first-generation

---

40 Seriously, go check out that book: Bessel van der Kolk, *The Body Keeps the Score: Brain, Mind, and Body in the Healing of Trauma* (New York: Penguin Publishing Group, 2015).

student, started her career at McKinsey, and received two master's degrees from Stanford University. While she looked perfect on paper, she struggled with her mental health during her teenage years. When she cried, her dad would yell, "No one is dead—save your tears for when I die." When she shared her suicidal thoughts with her mom, the first reply she got was, "How can you be so selfish?" She unconsciously believed that "because you are a teenager, that's what you are supposed to feel."[41]

Grace's trauma dated back to her parents and grandparents. Grace's mom grew up under the shadow of debt collectors coming to her door and looking for debts owed by Grace's grandpa. Even though Grace never had to face the violent debt collectors, she was really afraid of debt. Watching her parents struggle financially, she desperately wanted to get the best job with the most money. Even though Grace's parents never explicitly asked her to achieve anything, Grace wanted to prove that she was good enough for her dream schools. She achieved everything she could and was admitted early to Yale.

"I cannot remember a time when my home was worry-free," Grace told me. "My parents didn't know mental health was actually a problem." Grace shared the history of her trauma when interviewed in a *New York Times* article: "My parents wanted a better life for me, but they didn't know that the scars of their childhood traumas could still cause pain."[42]

---

41 Charlene Wang and Juhan," Issue #61 - Talk Show Spotlight - Grace Chiang, Founder of Cherish Parenting," LivingOS Newsletter, October 15, 2020.

42 Grace Chiang, "Healing the Whole Family," The New York Times, September 22, 2020.

She inherited her parents' trauma, yet she didn't know what she was going through was called "depression."

It was not until her friend committed suicide in college that Yale required her to see a therapist. She kept the visits a secret from her family and quietly began her healing journey. She started journaling and meditation. Through her practice, she noticed a familiar pattern throughout her family history and recentered herself by taking a few deep breaths. That was the moment when she discovered the real power of therapy. That was the moment when she began to process her emotions differently.

By healing and embracing her trauma, Grace dealt with her emotions.

4.

What made their stories complicated are intergenerational trauma and cultural conditioning.

Janet and Grace's parents did not know how to deal with their own wounds. We can either break this cycle or allow these wounds to restrict our lives.

While we cannot undo what has happened to our parents, we can accept that our parents tried their best. While we might not like it, we can cultivate empathy to understand what they have been through and start a productive dialogue. It takes time to heal from trauma, but we cannot delay the work. We need to engage our parents in difficult conversations. These conversations can feel incredibly uncomfortable, painful, or rejection filled. Therapists often say that the strong feeling is a cue to know that you are on the right track. Be curious and get under the message. That's how we can identify how our parents' traits have affected our lives and change the narrative we tell ourselves about who we are and who we can be.

While Grace and Janet have both explored their own trauma and inhabit their feelings, many other Chinese Americans are still struggling with mental health and self-expression. Dr. van der Kolk found that when your caregivers regularly neglect your needs, the emotional damage would be compounded. Your caregiver's behavior becomes a baseline for what to expect in life. You begin to expect that others will poorly treat you. As a coping strategy, you begin to reject a part of yourself, withdraw from social interactions, and believe that your feelings do not matter.[43]

In addition to intergenerational trauma, we are not culturally conditioned to express our feelings. As Stanford Professor Jeanne Tsai finds, the ideal emotional state of the Chinese culture is calm and composed, which is the opposite of the excitement and enthusiasm we like in American culture.[44] This cultural difference explains part of the gap in emotional awareness. Emotions are "biological signals designed to nudge you in the direction of beneficial change," as the *New York Times* bestselling author Mark Manson wrote in *The Subtle*

---

43 van der Kolk, *The Body Keeps the Score.*

44 Jeanne L. Tsai, "Ideal Affect: Cultural Causes and Behavioral Consequences," Perspectives on Psychological Science 2 (2007): 242–59.

*Art of Not Giving a F*ck.*[45] If emotion is not encouraged in the first two years of our lives, how could we cultivate the muscle to express what we think and be our authentic selves?[46]

When I reached out to interview Chinese Americans for *Model Breakers*, many people told me that I was the first person ever to ask about their stories. Outside of family, our stories are often hidden from society; kept private because they didn't know why they matter. *Have we all been conditioned to believe that we are not important? Have we all internalized that our stories should not be told?*

I am afraid that our silence made us a victim of society's ignorance and marginalized our collective political status early in life.

5.

Besides getting in touch with our emotions, we also need to embrace our identities.

Growing up in Taipei, I was lucky enough to learn history from people who looked like me. Yet even with the eighteen years of Chinese education, I still struggled with my identity during my first college year. When someone would ask me, "Where are you from?" I would feel exposed that I was an

---

45 Mark Manson, *The Subtle Art of Not Giving a F*ck* (San Francisco: HarperOne), 2016, p. 40, Kindle.

46 E.E. Werner and R.S. Smith, *Overcoming the Odds: High Risk Children from Birth to Adulthood* (Ithaca, NY, and London: Cornell University Press, 1992).

outsider. Growing up, no one asked where I was from. It was hard to answer this question properly.

More often than not, I had to give an unsatisfactory answer in the interest of time. Later I learned that questions like, "What is your background?" and "What is your ethnicity?" are microaggressions, especially toward Chinese Americans who desperately wanted to brush off their ethnicity. Yet, I didn't know better at the time. I was confused and found it hard to explain my cultural heritage in one sentence.

So, where am I from? I am ethnically Chinese. I was born in Australia. I grew up in Taipei. Unfortunately, these long, inconclusive answers generate more questions than answers. Any other simplified version would dishonor some crucial parts of me. Whenever I paused and asked the person, "Where do you think I am from?" I would get a perplexed look as if I should have figured that out already. Am I the only one who cannot articulate my identity?

Why are we often ridiculed or judged based on our looks?

6.

Multi-identities often create a cognitive dissonance when our external and internal racial identities don't match. While society often assigns us the racial identity we physically resemble, it might not represent how we are raised. I also fell into this trap when I first met my friend Irene in person.[47]

---

47 I've changed their name and identifying details.

Irene and I first connected online and later met up in San Francisco. When a girl walked toward me in the coffee shop, I did a double take. I didn't expect to meet someone, with Adler as her last name, to look purely Chinese. "People generally assume who I am." Irene later told me she was born in China and adopted by her Caucasian parents at a very young age.

Irene's Chinese heritage and Caucasian upbringing created a feeling of dissonance. Growing up in the Bay Area, she often got asked by Asian kids, "Do you speak Mando or Canto?" She didn't know what Mando or Canto meant. While Irene is ethnically Chinese, she was raised in a white family with white values. She didn't see herself as part of the racial group that looked like her. When Irene admitted that she identified with whiteness, her friend was confused: "Wait, but you're not white." Not knowing how to explain this dissonance, she wondered, "Am I crazy here?"

Through my interviews, I learned that people identify themselves with the predominant race they grew up with, regardless of their ethnicity. During the age when everyone wants to fit in, kids often mirror their peers. Even though the new identity conflicts with their value systems, they are socially pressured to fit in.

Irene thought of herself as white because that's the culture she was most familiar with. "I see racial identity as something connected to my cultural background," Irene said. "By that definition, it only made sense for me to identify as white because I grew up with white culture. I don't have the Asian cultural background that people think I do when they see me."

Irene's experience is the polar opposite of mine because she didn't grow up around people who "look" like her. Irene's story not only highlights the challenge of the global adoption complex, but that American society would define us by our ethnicity—even though that conflicts with how we choose to identify ourselves.

7.

Self-awareness gets tricky when we have multiple labels.

My friend Anthony Chen told me how much he hated explaining himself to everyone. He found that there was pressure to identify as American in the States, so he would just pick the most convenient label. Sometimes he is Taiwanese. Sometimes he is American. He told me, "I cannot change people's minds. Better to be open-minded and talk in other people's language." This identity-switching is a common experience among us third culture kids—children who spend a prominent part of their childhood outside of their parents' homeland.[48]

Identity switching and code-switching are common among multilingual speakers. Code-switching is often used by people who change how they speak or act to fit in with people around them.[49] The constant switching and wanting to fit in makes us lose sight of becoming more of ourselves. It is dangerous

---

48 D.C. Pollock and R.E. Van Reken, *Third Culture Kids: Growing Up Among Worlds* (Boston: Nicholas Brealy, 1999).

49 Matt Thompson, "Five Reasons Why People Code-Switch," NPR (NPR, April 13, 2013).

to internalize the perceptions of others. My friend Amy Deng would strategically switch between different identities based on the environment she found herself in. Sometimes it's even subconscious. In my experience, for example, I played the humble Asian stereotype when the angel investor questioned why I was in the room.

"When people ask me where I am from, I would just say Chicago." Amy, who left China and came to Chicago with her mom at fifteen, would change her answer based on the person who asked the question. Perhaps she got insecure about being who she was or was just tired of being "exotic." I once met a guy who told me I was exotic, which made me extremely uncomfortable. Calling someone else "exotic" meant you see yourself as the "origin." Calling someone "exotic" is an assertion of cultural superiority, stereotypes, and objects. Either way, Amy hoped that "Chicago" would shield her from the stereotypes against international students. She hid a part of her identity so that she could fit into the social norm. This strategy served her well until people talked about their childhood stories in America, which she had no connection with. That's when she would admit her full identity—the Chinese identity she had been secretly keeping to herself.

Amy's behavior stresses Chinese immigrants' tendency to switch their identity as a coping mechanism to fit in with American society. "I wrote about my struggle in my college application essay." Amy was a sophomore at UC Berkeley at the time of our interview and told me, "I talked about how I became proud of my identity even though I wasn't fully there." She was struggling with her Chinese identity. She was struggling to accept and explore her true self. Code-switching has become a convenient way to hide our identity and make us less of ourselves. Code-switching is a slippery slope to deny a part of who we are.

Although Amy struggled with code-switching, she surpassed the struggle and rose above it in a life-changing way. She has found a way to use identity in the startup world. For example, she was able to offer her network and startup experiences in Beijing to the Silicon Valley tech scene, and vice versa. This unique combination prompted her to start a newsletter on the Chinese market and affirmed her voice. This new skillset gave her the confidence to value her strengths and cherish her multiple identities.

8.

To overcome these self-imposed limitations, we first need to know more about ourselves. By knowing who we are and how we feel, we can think for ourselves and question society's standards. In an ideal world, self-awareness can help us survive and thrive. However, we are living in a world where we are constantly stereotyped. We need to know ourselves and speak up for ourselves.

To know who you are, you need to start by embracing your emotions and multiple identities.

Here are two exercises to get you started:

EXERCISE 1

EMBRACE YOUR EMOTIONS

Identify a specific moment that triggered your emotion. What happened?

____

____

____

____

What were you mostly feeling? Label the emotions with a simple word such as sad, mad, glad, or bad.

____

Acknowledge that these feelings can be tough. Remember, emotions make us human.

How would you respond if you are coming from your most resourceful place?

____

____

____

____

While we cannot cancel the emotions, we can decide where we spend our attention and how we want to respond. I found it more empowering to replace the fear with love and kindness.

What were you thinking at the moment? How do those thoughts help you become the person who you want to be?

____

____

____

____

These questions can help you see the connection between your thoughts and emotions.

EXERCISE 2

EMBRACE YOUR MULTIPLE IDENTITIES

Write down your multi-identities and the cultures that influenced the way you see the world.

____

____

____

____

For example, I am ethnically Chinese. I was born in Australia. I grew up in Taipei. I am raised to be rationally optimistic and see the sky as my limit.

Look at your identities. How have those identities served you? In both good and bad ways. Remember that everything is a double-edged sword.

For example, the Western culture encourages me to be brave, seek opportunities, and embrace who I am. The Eastern culture encourages me to be modest and evaluate where I am good enough.

What new possibilities would you unlock when you embrace all your identities?

For example, I can combine my Western and Eastern values to take calculated risks and share my experiences with people who have been in the same situation.

The work of knowing yourself is going to be a continual process. You will continually evolve as you begin the work to embrace your emotions and identities.

Remember that no labels can define us.

We define ourselves.

CHAPTER 5

BE YOURSELF

Dear Warren,

Have you ever felt that you are not enough?

1.

In Fall 2015, Amy Deng found herself in a scary cafeteria at Deerfield High School in Illinois. The tables were separated by different friend groups. Even though everyone is free to sit anywhere, the implicit social norm requires people to sit with their friend groups. Amy traced the noise and found a popular group of girls wearing jean jackets and Converse. They were laughing loudly like the *Friends* characters in the Central Perk Café and sharing food as if they were on a picnic. "Popular girls in my school were always really dramatic, loud, and cutting each other off," Amy recalled her first impression. "There is no way I could be friends with them." She felt like an outsider and felt the need to be someone else to be accepted. She wasn't sure whether she would change herself, but she had a hunch that she might become one of those kids who sit alone with their phones on the bench outside of the cafeteria.

While others loudly sat in laughter, she quietly sat in silence. While others shared food across the table, she had no idea how to start a conversation. Whenever people talked to her, she noticed that the small talks were stuck in the "nice" level. She would get a lot of curious questions about schools and food in China, and those conversations usually ended with people laughing at her broken English. Even though no one bullied her, she felt marginalized. She thought she could never find close friends. She didn't know why it was so hard to fit in. She became obsessed over the way she dressed, looked, and spoke. When she finally came up with a good sentence, it was already too late!

"It took me a year to convince myself that my English is good enough." When I asked Amy how she felt at that time, she said, "It's just what it is." She didn't know what she did wrong and why she was not accepted. Even though she knew she should be proud of herself, she was scared that being herself would leave her alone. Sometimes she would talk and laugh loudly even though she didn't know what she was laughing at. Sometimes she would act as if she was busy with social media by scrolling through Google search results. She experimented with every personality but her own.

Years after Amy graduated from Deerfield, she came to accept that she might never master all the English slang. "Not until I accepted the fact that my English will never be perfect did I start to believe that my English is good enough." Amy overcame her limiting belief and cherished the gift that she could learn something new about this country, this culture, and this language every single day.

2.

Chinese immigrants, myself included, grew up seeing our parents work really hard to get to where they are. Even though they have achieved certain success, they still work through late nights and weekends. Growing up under such influence, I found myself subconsciously wanting to work harder to prove myself. Even though I have gotten myself to a comfortable place, I can still feel the impulse of wanting to work harder.

As I asked myself why I continued to push myself to work harder, I noticed the pattern that Chinese immigrants were pressured to be anything but their true selves. I internalized the traditional view of success. I was optimizing for status and recognition. I chose to interview at the most competitive companies in the world because I wanted to prove myself. I thought happiness was about achieving more. I thought I could acquire happiness as I climbed up the social ladder.

However, I wasn't happy after achieving all of my goals. In 2018, I invested in coaching and looked inwards. I started to keep a daily journal, meditate twice a day, and study neuroscience to learn more about our brain. I began to investigate my wanting with these three questions:

1. Where does my wanting come from?
2. How has my self-identity restricted my wanting?
3. How have my culture and society influenced my wanting?

As I began to ask myself these questions, I noticed voices that came from my parents and family. Even though no one had explicitly asked me to achieve any goal, I made up my mind by looking at the people who got the most attention in class and media. I didn't know what success meant to me, so I copied the criteria used by my mentors, assuming there was a universal success criterion and they had figured it out.

I ended up chasing a career success formula that would over-index on the network, but I forgot to ask myself what I wanted to do with my life.

3.

It took me two years of intensive coaching, reflection, and life experiments to honor my wants and cultivate the courage to live my dream. When I took power back from social conditioning, I no longer had to wait for anyone to justify my happiness.

In a recent podcast interview, I uncovered my childhood dream of becoming a creator.[50] When I was eight, I dreamed about adding a *Hannah Montana* secret closet or a *Harry Potter* secret library in my room. This early desire made me want to be an interior designer. When family friends asked me, "What do you want to be when you grow up?" I would

---

50 Joyce Bao and Charlene Wang, "Charlene Wang, Permission to Become a Model Breaker," December 16, 2020, in *Permission to Become*, produced by Joyce Bao, podcast, 43:49.

confidently say, "Interior designer!"[51] My mom took me to learn the craft at drawing schools. A few years later, I began to lose interest because I found it too tedious. I eventually gave up my first dream.

Fifteen years later, I found myself back at the drawing board, replacing the brush with a keyboard.

Since the start of the COVID-19 pandemic, I published one article every day. I began with an advice blog for my bridesmaid Evelyn. She just ended a long-distance relationship and was asking for advice. I wanted to share my experience with her. I didn't feel ready, but I knew Evelyn would benefit from hearing my story. I had something to say and someone to read my work, so I leaped to publish my first article on making long-distance relationships work. Sometimes the world needs to hear your voice before you are ready.

I had been dreaming of writing since 2016. I wanted to write about my loneliness and relentless pursuit of success. However, I didn't have the confidence to put myself out there. I waited for four years to see if this body of knowledge would magically turn into wisdom. I had collected so much stuff that my first eighty essays were purely from my notes.

I ended up publishing 270 articles in 2020.[52] The magic happened when I shifted my focus from the outcome to the

---

51 My grandma later told me about her passion in interior design, which made me question whether this passion has been in my blood. It may be an early influence too because I was raised by my grandma.

52 Charlene Wang, "Issue #95 - LivingOS 2020 Year in Review," LivingOS Newsletter (LivingOS, December 26, 2020).

process. Instead of focusing on impressing people who barely knew who I was, I turned to write the way I lived my life. I followed my curiosity and wrote about topics I genuinely cared about. I wanted to bring inspiration and empower people to start something impactful in their lives.

As I write this book to you, I am also writing to my current and future family. I want my future kids and grandchildren to read this book and know everything about what happened to my generation of people. Writing helped me realize I could find joy in any moment.

I learned to enjoy life unconditionally.

That's how I redefined success for myself and was able to live out my dream.

4.

Most of us are conditioned to think in a limiting way, not knowing that the beliefs are entirely made up by ourselves.

Each of the stories shed light on the struggles we faced to be fully ourselves.

I realized my immigrant friends shared my limiting beliefs. They would cling to the idea that "they are not good enough." As Cathy Park Hong writes about her feeling as an Asian American in her book *Minor Feelings*, "My ego is in free fall while my superego is boundless, railing that my existence is not enough, never enough, so I become compulsive in my efforts to do better, be better, blindly following this country's gospel of self-interest, proving my worth by expanding my net worth, until I vanish."[53] This is the notion of passing into whiteness where a person blends in with another group and compromises their own identity.

Limiting beliefs come from many places. As immigrants, we gave up parts of our identity as we moved from one home to another. Thirty-three thousand Chinese students came to American high schools in 2016.[54] Three hundred sixty-nine thousand and five hundred students came for college and advanced degrees in 2018.[55] While it is easy to marvel at the sheer volume, we may not recognize the prevalence of losing and navigating our identity at a young age. Through my interviews, I realized that every Chinese Immigrant, regardless of background, has struggled to embrace their culture while taking in a new one.

I identify with both American confidence and Chinese filial piety. Like my friends, I do not fit in any single label, as I don't perfectly represent any prescribed profile. I see the same hesitation across other international students in college. When I asked my college friend Murong Xu, she told me she saw herself as a global citizen. She struggled to fully identify with Chinese even though she was born and raised in Beijing.

---

53 Hong, *Minor Feelings*, 35.

54 Simon Montlake, "For Chinese High-Schoolers, There's Value to Living and Learning in Iowa," The Christian Science Monitor (The Christian Science Monitor, October 4, 2018).

55 Bethany Allen-Ebrahimian, "The Number of Chinese Students at US Universities Has Nearly Tripled over the Past Decade," Axios, April 29, 2020.

Perhaps all these years of American education have made her a third-culture kid—children who spend a significant part of their childhood outside of their parents' homeland. Research shows that third-culture kids are more likely to speak at least two languages, have a broader world view, and are more culturally aware. At the same time, they often struggle with "homelessness," as their home is everywhere and nowhere.

I was curious about whether kids who came to the States earlier would feel any different during the formative years of high school. I reached out to Yuji Lai, who parachuted from China to stay with her host family in Albany, NY.

To my surprise, Yuji struggled relatively more than other international students I interviewed. In her first year, kids who knew so little about China hurt her. They asked her questions like, "Do you have iPads in China?" She told me how much these subtle, naïve assumptions culminated in her identity crisis: "It's okay to admit that you don't know about certain cultures or make stereotypical jokes, but it's another story when you speak assertively as if you have insights into another person's culture or country." These "stupid" stereotypes made her question who she was. But why would these "stupid" stereotypes make her question who she was? I later learned that no matter the assertions, no matter how ridiculous, would stay rent free in your head until a strong landlord came to brush it away. It turned out that kids who came earlier also struggled with finding a home in the States.

Similar to Murong, Yuji struggled to make sense of the new world she found herself in. She didn't want to change herself, play sports, or binge-watch *The Office*. She didn't understand why she couldn't be as popular as before. In addition, Yuji was pressured to prove herself. Like other Chinese immigrants, Yuji quit a top high school and convinced her family to spend fifty times more on her education tuition. The financial cost put a lot of pressure on her to succeed, no matter what. "Sometimes people, including my host family, can't understand why I was so stressed out and constantly working. I came here, and I have to do good."

5.

The American society is not the only source that pressures Chinese immigrants to fit in. There is another, perhaps more inherent, source of pressure that comes from our families. To justify this huge investment and transition, we had the pressure to work hard and make this investment worthwhile. For some reason, we all feel indebted to the sacrifice our parents made for us. For Chinese Americans, they have the pressure to make their parents' American Dream come true. For Chinese Immigrants, we had the pressure to make our "gamble" count. This is especially challenging for immigrant kids who have to figure out the rules and excel in society all at once.

Like many Chinese students, she chose a STEM major that would give Chinese Immigrants two more years of work visa as well as career prospects. Data shows that 50 percent of Asians major in business, sciences, or engineering. This trend shows that most people are choosing majors that could get a job or conforming to the norm. Interestingly, I ended up majoring in all of them during college—applied math, economics, and computer science.

While studying computer science at the University of Washington, Yuji met other popular, hardworking Asians like her. "Just having people facing the same amount of anxiety and stress made me feel normal again," she said. This shared feeling made her realize that it was cool to be hard-working and she didn't have to change herself. However, it was not until Yuji got her first internship that she could look beyond the basic needs and think about what she wanted in life. While this internship conveniently helped her build confidence, she struggled to find her true self. This real self was different from what the model minority expected her to be. Since then, she graduated from the University of Washington and rethought what she really wanted in life.

Such an illusion plays a critical role in American society. The idea that equates hard work with success is a central part of the American Dream. It is a grand vision that attracts generations of immigrants to leave their country, work hard, and bootstrap their way toward success. Indeed, we have all heard of the success story of a relative who came to the States with bad English, ground through many jobs, and made their way up the social ladder.

And here I am, a victim of the hard-working myth. I am the first one in my family to leave home and attend college in the States. I got a 2300 SAT score and a decent TOEFL score. Yet I wasn't able to clearly express myself in English. I had to rely on the writing center and friends to proofread my crappy essays. Nevertheless, I hustled hard and fortunately got my dream internship in Silicon Valley in the first year. I thought after I proved myself, I could gain my way toward happiness. However, I wasn't happy after achieving all my goals.

At the same time, I have seen many dreams fall flat because such success requires us to become someone else. And even if we compromise, it does not guarantee success. I know many people who came from a similar background, worked very hard, but still struggled to navigate their way. This got me to think that it might not be as simple as "work hard and you will succeed."

6.

The American Dream is just a dream. It doesn't have to be your dream.

The term American Dream was first coined by historian James Truslow Adams in his bestselling book *Epic of America* as "that dream of a land in which life should be better and richer and fuller for everyone, with opportunity for each according to ability or achievement."[56] Is opportunity truly equal?

I can't help but look at Asian American role models and see a similar ambivalence toward the American Dream. Laura Huang, preeminent Harvard Business School professor and author of *Edge*, quoted her parents in one of our recent conversations: "If you put in the hard work, it will speak for itself." However, she quickly realized that hard work itself was not enough and systematic injustice was real. For instance, she was denied admission to an advanced class even when she got the highest test scores. In addition, the teachers had her take

56 James Truslow Adams, *The Epic of America*, Transaction Publishers, May 1, 2012.

ESL classes even though she grew up in the States. Despite being passed on and held to double standards, she studied and turned stereotypes into her advantage.

When Laura completed her Ph.D. in Management at UC Irvine, she attended the career fair where she had to compete with other graduates from Harvard and Stanford. She didn't have any publications, prestigious institutions, or famous advisors, so she needed to redefine the faculty's perception of her. "I realized that the perceptions they would have about me are around competence," Laura told me. "I had people ask me questions about my dissertation, which was very much out of the box." By owning her own story, she became a professor, mentored underprivileged kids, and shared her playbook in her book *Edge*.[57] Laura's story teaches us the importance of recognizing that we are already enough. Once we acknowledge our greatness, we can decide how we want to invest our efforts. If you are going to work hard, why not invest the time and energy in what you really want?

Now you may wonder, "If the American Dream is just a dream, why are people still holding onto this distant ideal?" One explanation is the system justification theory by psychologist Josh Jost, which suggests that people who have benefited from a particular system see that system as fair, even if there are clear problems.[58] If the people who write the law and run the country rise through the ranks with the American Dream, why would they demolish the foundation that made them who they are today?

---

57 Huang, *Edge*.

58 John T. Jost, "A Theory of System Justification," American Psychological Association (June 2017).

If you feel that whatever keeps the American Dream alive is not serving you, remember that you can always define your own dream. The truth is that following the American Dream, or any dreams created by others, may not make you happy. Why would you expect somebody else's dream to work for you? They at best serve the people who come from similar backgrounds or live in the same circle. If you would like to attain success, start taking responsibility for the goals you pursue. You are in charge of your destiny. You are in charge of your life. Stop complaining about the mismatched reality. Start creating your own dreams.

Just like historian James Truslow Adams who coined the term "American Dream," you can create your own dream too.

7.

Our limiting beliefs from the immigrant experience, the Asian culture, and the American Dream reinforced the idea that we are not enough. Each story in this chapter sheds light on the different limiting beliefs we imposed on ourselves. Once we break this limiting belief, we can follow our interests and live out our full life.

Rarely are we ever told that happiness is within our control.

The rigid expectations are set up in a way to make society happy. If we go to school and get good grades, we will be rewarded by our parents and teachers. We try to act like others because we want to be accepted by our peers. We try to follow the rules because we want to be praised by our parents. We are trained to make everyone happy at the expense of our destiny.

I asked my cousin Amelia why she worked so hard to satisfy everyone. She told me she just wanted to make her family proud of her: "I want to make myself happy, but I put my family first. Family is everything to me. The happiness of my parents will then reflect on me, so I'll be happy." The question I didn't ask is "What about you? When is your turn? When are you ready to serve yourself?"

Here are three steps to help you start to be who you want to be:

EXERCISE

STEP 1: TAKE STOCK OF YOUR NEEDS

How much income do you need to survive? Start by adding your rent, utilities, and regular bills.

____

____

____

____

Once you figure out how to get food on the table, you can shift your focus from being haunted by the scarce resources to reflecting on what you really want in life.

STEP 2: IDENTIFY YOUR PROBLEMS

What problems would you like to solve now? Why do these problems exist? Keep asking yourself why until you get to the root cause.

____

____

____

____

By identifying the root cause, you can break out of the autopilot and examine your limiting beliefs.

STEP 3: CREATE YOUR DREAM

How can you create a dream that feels more authentic to you?

____

____

____

____

Once you write out your dream, you will know whether you are working to please yourself or someone else. Remember that we are enough to be who we want to be. We have everything we need to start living out the dream already.

By embracing these advanced mindsets, you will smash the American Dream and create the vehicle to define your own success. By being yourself, you will smash the model minority and become a model breaker.

I was eager to be part of the American Dream, but not anymore.

I am enough to become my wildest dream.

CHAPTER 6

TELL YOUR OWN STORY

Dear Warren,

Before our stories are picked up by history, we need to tell them ourselves. Because if we don't, who will?

1.

In 2011, the nine-person dance group Girls' Generation performed at the Madison Square Garden in New York. Every seat in the 20,000-person arena was sold out.[59] Their 2009 single hit video "Gee" has been viewed 266 million times on YouTube. Sunny of Girls' Generation told Grammy that "when they performed in Los Angeles, New York and Paris,

59 Jacob Moore, "K-Pop Takes Over Madison Square Garden," (Complex, April 20, 2020).

we were shocked and surprised to see that the majority of our fans were non-Asian."[60]

K-pop's growth and influence have skyrocketed since then.

In 2012, Psy took the horse dance viral. His music video "Gangnam Style" has been viewed over 3.9 billion times on YouTube.[61]

In 2020, the world's most popular band BTS's latest album *Dynamite* was at the top of Billboard Global for eight weeks straight.[62] Their music video "DNA" and "Boy With Luv" have been viewed more than 1.1 billion times on YouTube.[63][64]

BTS's repeated hits have marked K-pop's transition from teen fandom to role models. They have taken self-expression to another level, performed excellent choreography, and used music to tell their stories powerfully. Not only is BTS breaking boundaries in the world of pop music, but it is also creating a community and making its members feel like they have a voice.

"Tell me your story. I want to hear your voice, and I want to hear your conviction," BTS's leader Kim Nam-joon addressed at the United Nations. "No matter who you are, where you're

---

60 Jon Matsumoto, "How K-Pop's US Popularity Is Exploding," GRAMMY.com (Recording Academy, August 27, 2020).

61 "PSY - GANGNAM STYLE(강남스타일) M/V," July 15, 2012, video, 4:12.

62 Gary Trust, "BTS' 'Dynamite' Adds to Record Run Atop Billboard's Global Charts," Billboard, January 11, 2021.

63 *Big Hit Labels*, "BTS (방탄소년단) 'DNA' Official MV," September 18, 2017, video, 4:15.

64 *Big Hit Labels*, "BTS (방탄소년단) '작은 것들을 위한 시 (Boy With Luv) (feat. Halsey)' Official MV," April 12, 2019, video, 4:12.

from, your skin color, gender identity, speak yourself."[65] Their message about spreading love and identity has struck a chord with youth worldwide.

This is an example of how the world embraced who we are. Just like Kim Nam-joon, you can speak for yourself too.

2.

We can manifest storytelling in music, art, poetry, business, and writing. The stories we tell ourselves define who we are.

However, telling a story can be challenging.

Maggie Yip is a college student at the University of British Columbia. Her parents were first-generation immigrants from China and came to have Maggie and her brothers in Vancouver, Canada. She has been very open about sharing her own story. She reached out to me on LinkedIn when I first shared my research project for *Model Breakers*. I had no idea of the powerful story I was going to hear from her.

"My parents both sacrificed a lot to raise us," Maggie told me. "My dad was busy working as a chef, and my mom was busy raising my brothers and me." When Maggie first got diagnosed with attention-deficit/hyperactivity disorder (ADHD) and obsessive-compulsive disorder (OCD) in fourth grade, her parents didn't follow up with the proper treatments. They

65 Bard Wilkinson, "K-Pop Band BTS Tells World Youth to 'Speak Yourself' at UN," CNN (Cable News Network, September 25, 2018).

didn't know how to help her navigate the challenges because they never learned about mental illness.

When Maggie turned sixteen, her ADHD and OCD manifested into chronic depression and generalized anxiety. She wanted to get help, but she didn't know how to tell people her story. She quietly arranged the counseling and doctor's appointments in between classes. "I did all this on my own," Maggie said to me softly. "My friends in elementary school bullied me, so I didn't know how to trust people in my social circle."

After taking the doctor's prescription for months, Maggie wanted to challenge this taboo topic in the Chinese culture:

> **Maggie**: *No matter how hard I work, it is tough for me to focus.*
>
> **Maggie's mom:** *Oh, it's because you're always on the computer or you're always going out.*

Maggie was frustrated by how her mom rejected her feelings, so she showed her mom the orange pill bottle to prove that at least someone—her doctor—believed that she needed help. Her mom was livid.

> **Maggie's mom:** *Why are you taking the medication?*
>
> **Maggie:** *Because I am struggling with my mental health.*
>
> **Maggie's mom:** *But there's nothing wrong with you.*

It was hard for Maggie's mom to accept that her daughter was mentally sick.

Maybe she was afraid that the drug would lead to addiction and losing her daughter. Or perhaps she didn't want to feel like a bad mother who failed her daughter by making her go through such emotional challenges.

3.

Her mom's denial was devastating for Maggie, but Maggie didn't give up. Her will to recover was stronger than her mom's resistance to trust her feelings.

She took the medicine at school, arranged private therapy sessions, and challenged her negative self-talk with cognitive behavioral therapy. She went from surrendering her power to taking responsibility for her life at nineteen.

While her mom's denial once made her depression worse, Maggie accepted her mom's reactions as she learned more about her parents' cultural values such as honor, respect, and saving face. In Chinese culture, it is weak to show emotion or weakness. Challenges are a natural part of life, and they all shall pass. While such a mindset has empowered generations of immigrants to survive, this very same mindset also made Maggie's parents believe she needn't share her experiences or seek external help.

"Living with mental health challenges is something that most don't understand unless they go through it themselves,"

Maggie told me. "I would rather my mom have not understood me than to have her experience such a thing." While Maggie stopped sharing with her mom, she started to open up about her story with others. She knew that sharing her story would make other people feel less alone.

Now that Maggie has recovered, she opened up these conversations with her friends who are now coming out of the woodwork. "A number of people reach out to me to talk about their mental health challenges," Maggie messaged me. "They believed I would understand and know what to say." A few of those people had never previously confided in anyone. She would also reach out when her friends and acquaintances shared their stories online. As she heals her mental health, she wants to make people feel more courageous and willing to embrace their own stories.

She told the new story with love and compassion.

4.

We all have the right to speak out and express ourselves. However, it can be scary to share our story. I was afraid that no one would be receptive to my story if I showed my true colors, so I asked my life coach Isabel for help:

> **Me:** *I am frustrated that I said nothing when my colleagues asked me what I did over the weekend. I minimized what I did because I was afraid to be seen as too intense.*
>
> **Isabel:** *Is there a lack of alignment that is whispering to you?*

Me: *Yes, I don't want to reveal that I am coaching high achievers, running a nonprofit, and writing a book on the weekends. I would love to be myself, but I'm okay because I have expressed myself through writing.*

Isabel: *Let's talk about the pros and cons of showing up as yourself.*

Me: *The pro is that I can share what I am doing authentically. The con is that I might make people who said they were relaxing on the weekend feel inadequate.*

I caught myself midway through the conversation because I noticed a thinking trap. I assumed that feeling great makes others feel worse. But even if I feel miserable, the world will not suffer less.

We can be empathetic and present without taking on their feelings. Suffering is not a prerequisite of being compassionate. We don't have to suffer at the same time. We don't have to be crazy about our successes when someone is suffering. We can still be compassionate without minimizing our joy.

Isabel: *Is there another possibility to share about the things you love?*

Me: *I can start by sharing one thing at a time. As I consciously choose to share my goodness, I will feel more aligned with who I am.*

When we repeatedly downplay our small wins, we allow this behavior to become a pattern. The key here is to know who we are and align our choices accordingly. Once you get in touch with your inner confidence, you may become honest with yourself.

Perhaps you say one thing, and nobody follows up. Then you can comfortably keep it to yourself because you are honoring their preference. On the other hand, when people get excited about what you said, you get to say more about what you want.

I traced my memory to see how this pattern showed up in my life.

Growing up, my dad was always proud of celebrating himself. He would chase the spotlight while my mom would stand in the shadow. My mom didn't like to have a profile picture and told me she didn't want anyone to know her. I never understood why she didn't want to be seen.

It took me a few years to realize that my mom was afraid to expose herself in public light because the low profile made her feel safe. Subconsciously, I mirrored her behavior and downplayed my success, yet this strategy did not align with who I am. Once I found this root cause, I stopped the excuse that "most people couldn't handle me." I started showing up consciously because I wanted to love and be myself.

As I shared my story, I got letters from readers sharing how my experience had inspired them to change their lives. These small wins showed that my message resonates, and I'm onto something bigger than my life.

Even though I may never feel ready, I will keep showing up because of the impact each message could create in our lives.

5.

There's one more thing to address before we tell our stories.

We first need to start by knowing the facts and knowing ourselves. Once we cultivate a sense of self-awareness, we can ground ourselves in the values that feel true. This self-awareness would build our trust and back us up when the world is not ready for us. There are going to be people out there who lack self-awareness and are insecure about themselves. When they project this insecurity upon you, they want to make you feel bad. When these haters hate, it says nothing about you and everything about them. They lack the self-awareness to face their fears, so they project that fear onto the stronger person in the room—you.

Theodore Roosevelt said in his popular "Citizenship in a Republic" speech, "It is not the critic who counts. The credit belongs to the man who is actually in the arena, who at the best knows in the end the triumph of high achievement, and who at the worst, if he fails, at least fails while daring greatly, so that his place shall never be with those cold and timid souls who know neither victory nor defeat."[66] I love how Brené Brown described those "cold and timid souls" as those who sit on the "cheap seats in the arena and never venture onto the floor."[67] If you are fighting with sweats and souls in the arena, why care about those cheap seats who have no real stakes in the awesome person you are becoming soon?

---

66 "Citizenship in a Republic," Speech at the Sorbonne, Paris, April 23, 1910 The Works of Theodore Roosevelt, Vol XIII, 506-529.

67 Brené Brown, *Rising Strong: How the Ability to Reset Transforms the Way We Live, Love, Parent, and Lead*, New York: Random House, 2017, kindle.

If you are playing for the long-term game, why bother those who will not stay with you till the end of the game?

With a decade of research, Brené Brown found that "vulnerability is the birthplace of love, belonging, joy, courage, empathy, and creativity. It is the source of hope, empathy, accountability, and authenticity."[68] It is vulnerable to show up as you are. It is okay to be scared about showing vulnerability. Hold on to what resonates with you. Even though someone doesn't like who you are, so be it. You cannot change them, but you can change your reaction to them.

There will always be people who like you and others who don't like you. The good news is that those negative voices have nothing to do with you. Once you know that it's just the eye of the beholder, you will become liberated. It is way too easy to criticize when you have no skin in the game. Here's another great reminder from Brené Brown: "If you're not in the arena also getting your ass kicked, I'm not interested in your feedback."[69]

The next time you feel hurt or this fear trickles up, pause when the judgment chimes in. Remind yourself of the people who you are serving. Think about the people you are going to help. Would you choose to please the cheap seats at the cost of helping people who you deeply care about? Channel those fears you feel into your vulnerability with love. Do it for you, for people who are going to appreciate you. Trust that people who need it will find you.

---

68 Brené Brown, *Daring Greatly: How the Courage to Be Vulnerable Transforms the Way We Live, Love, Parent, and Lead,* New York: Random House, 2012, 34.

69 Ibid.

As you invite more people into your world, you will get the opportunity to forge deeper connections. While sharing your true self and your own story can be vulnerable, every step counts. When you are not afraid to show people your true colors, you are giving yourself and others the permission to be vulnerable and human too. When you continue to honor who you are, this courage muscle will give you the confidence to shake it off like Taylor Swift.

You are worth being seen.

6.

I wanted to see whether Maggie is unique or part of a larger trend of others trying to rewrite their old story. I interviewed over fifty Chinese Immigrants and Chinese Americans at different stages in their lives. Through these interviews, I raised fundamental questions like:

- How do you see yourself?
- How do others see you?
- What culture do you identify with?
- How would you describe your identity to others?
- What was the most challenging moment in your life?
- How have you navigated that?

I am very moved by each person's deep stories yet struggled to find these stories in mainstream media. While most of their stories are hidden in the mainstream, I can feel their passion for life. After all, they have all reached out to me, a stranger on the internet, to document their beautiful stories. I can feel their desires to be heard. My job is to let their stories breathe and take a new life on their own.

Recently, a number of Hollywood movies have centered around Asian stories and included Asian actors. From movie director Jon M. Chu's *Crazy Rich Asians* to Lulu Wang's *The Farewell*, we see a new wave of media celebrating the cultural differences and difficulties we have to go through as Asian Americans.[70] [71] They gave us a sense of pride in the specialness.

When Constance Wu, the lead actress of *Crazy Rich Asians*, first started acting in New York, she found that most Asians were hired to add color around the lead white actor's story. At that time, the media was all about neutralizing Asians, and the directors wanted to be politically correct. While she knew that Asian representation was vital to her, she was too busy surviving the playing field and didn't have the luxury to think about it.

When Wu came to Hollywood, she saw a shift from being politically correct to be curious about differences.[72] The networks and producers need to differentiate themselves with a

---

70 Constance Wu, Henry Golding, Michelle Yeoh, and Gemma Chan. *Crazy Rich Asians*, dir by Jon M. Chu, Burbank, CA: Warner Bros. Pictures, 2018.

71 Lulu Wang, *The Farewell*, United States: A24, 2019.

72 *CAPE (Coalition of Asian Pacifics in Entertainment)*, "#IAm Constance Wu Story," May 7, 2015, video, 11:54.

different take. This new trend pushes the creators to be curious about experiences that speak to more audiences and bring diverse content to light. With *Crazy Rich Asians*, Constance joined the first all-Asian cast in twenty-five years to tell a story that helped us see more of ourselves.

Alongside this exciting trend of representation, Sandra Oh, best known as Cristina Yang on *Grey's Anatomy*, noted that "change is slow and that's okay. Because every day change has to happen in a much deeper and interior kind of way. When it is authentic to us, it will come."[73] What Sandra says is true because real change needs to start from ourselves. We need to do deep work to understand who we are, what feels true to us, and how we want to be perceived. It is tormenting to wait for the external structure to change. It is more empowering to seek change within ourselves and our community. It starts by telling our own story.

Storytelling is how we make sense of the world. These stories about family and culture contribute to the expectation that we should quietly paddle until we become successful someday. While this strategy may protect us from ridicule and "save face," it comes at the cost of understanding and connection. After all, we are connected through vulnerability, not success stories. If we could honor our unique struggles, we can redefine the stereotypes and reset the expectations others had for us. We can break the model minority and rewrite the folklore that we need to fulfill the model minority expectation set up to limit us, rather than empower us to be happy with our lives.

---

73 *CAPE (Coalition of Asian Pacifics in Entertainment)*, "#IAm Sandra Oh Story," May 18, 2018, video, 6:30.

Together, we can create a narrative that can show the world our strength and tell our beautiful story.

7.

Telling your story also shapes you into who you want to become. Through sharing your stories, you can connect with your community and uncover who you want to become.

Looking back on my life, I realized that I was once there, grinding through and puttering along with life. I was on the path to achieving more until I burned out. I was living to work, instead of working to live. Many hauntings held me back and inversely affected my life. I knew they were deep in my heart but had no idea how to deal with them. Even though I could pretend my life is colorful, I knew a part of me was dark and insecure.

Fortunately, I took a hard look at my life and decided to do something different. I began to write every day and built my company LivingOS along the way. I wrote down my thoughts and clarified my desire. I faced the hauntings and turned them into my superpower. I rewrote my story in a whole new voice, which would empower both my strengths and push my limits. Since then, I have learned to embrace myself fully. I am now working on something I am passionate about and coaching hundreds of high achievers through the LivingOS Fellowship.[74] The fellowship has inspired so many people to do the same.

---

74 LivingOS Fellowship is a group coaching experience for high achievers: www.livingos.org/fellowship.

One of our youngest fellows, Ashley Lin, shared in the final coaching session, "I have never experienced vulnerability with this demographic before. I used to reject my Taiwanese identity. My parents aren't super vulnerable. My immigrant community isn't super vulnerable either. I just never thought it was like a place where I could fit in, but this experience changed my mind around that. This made me a lot more hopeful of what we could achieve together." Ashley brought her breakthroughs and new stories to her community in Vancouver, Washington.

Through coaching and writing, I hope to help each of us break out of the intergenerational mold and lift each other at every stage of life.

You may have a story to tell but don't know how. Here's how you can start:

EXERCISE

STEP 1: UNDERSTAND HOW YOU ARE PERCEIVED

Ask your friends and colleagues to share five adjectives that would best describe you.

____

____

____

____

Once you understand how people see you, you can start from their baseline to rewrite your story.

STEP 2: UNDERSTAND THAT NEGATIVE PEOPLE ARE JUST HUMAN

When someone else is being negative, seek to understand them first through these two angles:

1. What are they avoiding? What are they trying to communicate?
2. What is the negative person trying to avoid in their own life?

____

____

____

____

You cannot control how people think of you, but you can choose to respond confidently to those who attack your value. Often, the negative people are just humans who don't know how to deal with their own problems. If you try to understand where they are coming from, you will feel less violated.

STEP 3: START FROM YOUR COMMUNITY

What story would you like to share with your friends? Write down your story below.

____

____

The more I learn about the Chinese community, the more hopeful I become. While I cannot predict how the future evolves, I know that if we continue to advocate for ourselves and share our stories with the world, positive changes will take place.

We need people to have a voice and make waves.

The world needs books like this. The world needs more activists. The world needs me and you.

Now is the time to tell your story.

CHAPTER 7

TAKE RISKS

Dear Warren,

I admire your conviction on taking the risks that seemed so far-fetched at times.

1.

Kelly Wang was born and raised in the Shanghai area as an only child. Even though she attended Chinese schools her whole life, she had an American Dream before knowing what America was about. She was fed up with the rigid knowledge transfer in China and longed for a well-rounded education. She wanted to think for herself; her constant questioning even got her the nickname "Miss Question." To fulfill her intellectual curiosity, she struck a deal with her parents: If she got into one of the top five colleges in China, her parents would support her to pursue a college education in the United States.

Indeed, Kelly ended up getting into Tsinghua University, the Harvard of China. It was unthinkable that any student would quit such a prestigious school to study abroad for most traditional Chinese families. Despite this, Kelly was determined to pursue her American Dream in higher education. "My parents were worried, but they couldn't stop me," Kelly said. "They were open-minded and progressive enough to support me."

While her parents had concerns, they saw how Kelly wanted to chase her dream. While most people couldn't understand why she would drop everything for an unknown future, she took the big gamble and transferred to Brown University. During her first year at Brown, she became the president of Brown Ballroom Club and mastered the art of dancing while managing a team. During her second year, she built financial models for Goldman Sachs' Private Equity Group as a summer intern. During her third year, she followed her interest and studied abroad in Amsterdam. During the final year, she secured prestigious full-time job offer at McKinsey. When her parents came for college graduation and saw her dreams realized, they finally understood why she took the leap and was very proud of her. Many years later, Kelly became my colleague at Google.

Just like Kelly, I challenged myself to leave my comfort zone in Taiwan and take a gamble at Brown. When I decided, I knew little about what was ahead of me, but I had a big dream. After all, I was raised to make the most out of everything.

Look, if I didn't take the risk to come to the States, I wouldn't have met the mentors that helped me get a head start in entrepreneurship. If I didn't take the risk to apply for jobs that seemed out of reach, I wouldn't have started my career with Google. If I didn't take the risk to share my thoughts online, I wouldn't have founded the LivingOS community that supported me every day. By taking small steps out of my comfort zone, I built up my risk appetite and courage toward the unknown. As Glennon Doyle said in *Untamed*, "The braver I am, the luckier I get."[75]

2.

As humans, we are wired to notice threats and weaknesses. While such genes have helped us survive the Stone Age, they have also made us extremely risk averse. While avoiding risk makes us feel safe, we often pay a high price for certainty. If we don't ask the hard questions to find out what we want and take the risk to change, we will eventually lose the spark and stagnate in life. If we focus on the risks associated with changes, we will be locked into the stability with fear. Stability is healthy when it serves your purpose, and it is not healthy when it doesn't; risks operate similarly.

One effective strategy to overcome risk aversion is to adopt the growth mindset I referenced in Chapter Two. When you believe you can develop intelligence and talent, you will be more willing to take risks, explore new opportunities, and experience success. On the other hand, people with the fixed mindset are often trapped in fear and avoid risks at all costs. Such risk aversion hinders their personal development and shuts down the wonder that could have happened in life. While doing nothing may feel like the safest decision, it only guarantees that you will miss opportunities to grow.

---

75 Glennon Doyle, *Untamed*, New York: Dial Press, March 10, 2020.

Another question I often ask myself is, "What would you do if you knew you wouldn't fail?" This question helps me uncover my true motivation because that's what matters at the end of the day. We are so often trapped in the expectation and status quo that we couldn't see the upside of risks. By asking this question, we could shift our focus to the beautiful journey and show up for ourselves even during the difficult moments in life. One of my core values is to deliver a meaningful impact to people who I care about. Knowing this value, I decided to focus on the founder-market fit of LivingOS.[76]

For example, it would've been a safe choice to focus on popular topics such as job interviews or career hacks. Instead, I tackled the big hairy problem—what does it take to live a good life—through small-group coaching. Even though the business could struggle to scale, this investment would still be worthwhile because everyone involved would be a lot more fulfilled. With little data and much conviction, I redirected the nonprofit's focus to serving one hundred fellows in 2021. This pivot turned out to be the best decision we've made.

The fear of taking risks has kept us stagnant for too long. To overcome our aversion to risk, we can focus on the upsides of changes. By doing so, we will increase our confidence and reduce the fear of uncertainty. The first step is to gather information. You can identify your change's costs and benefits by asking friends who have been through a similar change or reading case studies online. This information provides us with a tangible means for calculating the risks.

---

76 Charlene Wang, "Stop Asking For Product-Market Fit.," LivingOS (blog), July 5, 2020.

By making our fear rational, we can turn our fear of failure into taking action.

Whenever I told my coach that I was uncomfortable doing something, my coach would remind me just to do it. Little by little, these leaps of faith pulled me toward my desire and away from fear. I learned to replace the critical self-doubting voice with love. I became more open to share my thoughts, build a community, and experiment with life. As I took more risks, I realized we are a lot harder to break. We are more resilient than we thought.

Many scholars define resilience as the capacity to recover quickly from adversity. We can cultivate resilience by asking, *Is what I'm doing helping me or harming me?* By asking ourselves whether this risk is helping or hurting us, we would know whether the risk is beneficial to our growth. By choosing the pain that will push us to grow, we would become more resilient. The more resilient we are, the more we can choose to adapt to moments of change. When we repeatedly choose higher growth paths, we will build up our muscles to become stronger every day.

By taking small steps, we can start embracing new opportunities in life.

3.

Chinese Immigrants have taken an enormous risk to immigrate to the United States. Most people are like Candice Lee, who came without knowing what was ahead. Candice came to stay with her family in rural Maryland at fourteen. At that time, her extended family was running a Chinese restaurant and working every day. Seeing her family working so hard, Candice got to know the value of resilience and hard work. However, the hard work took a toll on their health. Being the only Asian community in rural Maryland, Candice's family didn't know how to reach out for help. Not only was their chronic health condition neglected but the children, Candice and her cousin, also internalized the helplessness growing up.

Being the new girl at school, Candice was very self-conscious of her accented English. She was shy and shameful about sharing her story with others. She was homesick. She lost her period for almost a year and lost a lot of weight, but she was too embarrassed to bring her condition up to anyone besides her mom. She desperately wanted to get out. She tried to take a gamble to improve her life.

Through a friend, Candice found a host family in California. After confirming through a virtual meeting, she applied for a high school transfer in the middle of the school year. When she brought up this California plan to her extended family, everyone was intimidated by the huge risk involved. Yet, Candice refused to give up. She spoke up about how she felt about school and her future. She told them about how she had to give up all her interests because no one could drive her to the after-school clubs. She shared how she was stuck at school and home. Candice knew the only way to be happy was to speak up for herself.

Candace broke away from her quiet stereotype and started a new life in the San Francisco Bay Area. With the support of her host family, she was free to do anything. She proactively reached out to student clubs and connected with the strong Asian community. On her weekend BART trips, she would explore San Francisco and volunteer at churches. Through volunteering services, she broke out of her social circle and began to learn about the challenges in everyone's life. If she didn't leap to leave her extended family in Maryland, she might never have found the confidence and community that would support her dreams. The risk of leaving home rewarded her with a whole new world of opportunities she couldn't have otherwise.

What would you be willing to risk in the name of your dreams?

4.

Every year, 85,000 skilled professionals receive the H1-B visa to work in the United States. This employer-sponsored program has brought in millions of talented professionals across mathematics, engineering, technology, and medical sciences since 1990. Jimmy Lin is one of those superstar software engineers who came to the US on H1-B.[77]

Jimmy was always learning and building something new. In seven years, he built the payment infrastructure for Facebook and Airbnb and became the industry's payment expert. In the back of his mind, he always wanted to apply his technical expertise and start something himself on his own. However, when I asked him why he was not going after the dream, he

77 I've changed their name and identifying details.

told me that he needed a non-technical co-founder—someone who could socialize his great ideas on his behalf. That reply surprised me because Jimmy always had a lot to say. Something seemed off.

After a few rounds of conversations, I noticed that Jimmy was quite insecure about his big dream. He held onto many limiting beliefs. For example, he would blame his inaction on his lack of a great degree. He mentioned that many startups pride themselves on their Ivy League background while other startups such as Reddit and Zoom have been just as successful otherwise. These limiting beliefs held Jimmy back from taking the risk to pursue his dream.

While it may sound ridiculous to keep these limiting beliefs, there is a reason why these beliefs live in our brains. They preserve our energy. They keep us in our comfort zone. They make us feel safe. In many ways, we are complicit in keeping these beliefs alive.

However, taking risks doesn't mean that you must leave your family like Candice Lee did or wave your sexuality around as Ali Wong does.

Do you have any areas in your life where you seem to have an invisible barrier? The good news is that you can rewire these beliefs too. If no one has ever challenged this way of thinking before, just know that you can dismantle those limiting beliefs and create a limitless way of thinking.

Here are three steps to help you incorporate these steps in life:

EXERCISE

STEP 1: SEPARATE THE LIMITING BELIEFS FROM REALITY

Find someone who is candid. Tell them your stories and ask them to tear apart your excuses.

For example:

1. *"I'm not ready." => Some people spend their entire lives waiting for the stars to get aligned. There is no such thing as "fully ready," so don't wait. You just need your permission to get started today.*

2. *"I'm not creative." => Everyone has something unique and valuable to share with the world. No one can tell your own story. Once you start putting your viewpoint out there, you will create the luck you need to move forward.*

3. *"All the good ideas are taken." => This might be the most common excuse. There are new products and startups featured on the news every day. You can start by taking notes of what captures your interest, and you will build your audience over time.*

STEP 2: TAKE SMALL, INCREMENTAL RISKS

Do something that scares you a little bit.

____

____

____

____

For example, you can send cold emails to people you admire. Share your thoughts online. Start a conversation with strangers. The goal is to take a step forward from where you are and take as many shots as possible along the way. As you build up the pool of opportunities, you will see beyond your limits and start creating new opportunities for yourself.

STEP 3: IDENTIFY NEW OPPORTUNITIES

Where can you take more risks in your life? Where would you like to receive more rewards?

____

____

____

____

Identify one risk you are willing to take this year and prepare yourself for it. Don't be afraid to try new things. Focus on the upside of the changes instead.

As Ralph Waldo Emerson said, "All life is an experiment."[78] The more risks you take, the better.

Gradually, we can create a new world that is more welcoming and empowering to ourselves.

78 Ralph Waldo Emerson, Journals of Ralph Waldo Emerson, with Annotations - 1841-1844.

CHAPTER 8

BEING OKAY WITH NOT BEING OKAY

Dear Warren,

How can we embrace other people as they are?

1.

In November 1997, Tiffany Yu was involved in a car accident where she lost her dad and permanently paralyzed her right arm. She was nine years old. After the accident, she spent her childhood at doctor's appointments and coping with the trauma alone. It was particularly challenging because her mother acted as if the car accident never happened. To save face, her mother would make up for her father's absence by telling others that he was on business trips. Such toxic positivity forced a fake look in the family.

"My mom didn't provide an opportunity for me to heal," said Yu, now thirty-two, a Taiwanese American, and an avid disability advocate. "It took me twelve years before I spoke publicly about the car accident and what it did to me." It took her another six years to label what had happened as trauma and yet another two years to start healing with therapy.

Yu started her career in investment banking and is now serving the disability community with her community-centered business Diversability. "Creating Diversability is the biggest gift in life," Yu told me. "It has allowed me to explore my identity because I'm in a support group with people who share similar experiences of being socially isolated and excluded." While she has inspired people to embrace who they are and share their stories at TEDx and Davos, her mom is still unsupportive of her work.

Yu's mom always asks her when she would get a "real job." Even though Yu has become a role model for her community, she still struggles to be fully herself in front of her mom. Even though she has accomplished so much and changed so many lives, her work directly exposes the cultural stigma—death, disability, and trauma—her mom is deeply ashamed of. "I felt like fighting with a wall," Yu said. It is tricky to cross the cultural barrier. "It is the antithesis of what I was raised to do." Yu said, "I was raised to live from my head and achieve and be humble. Now, as a disabled Asian woman, I am standing out in every way my culture has told me not to." Yu struggled to have the first level of support from her mom. In fact, the more people she reaches, the more ashamed she makes her mom feel.

On Yu's thirtieth birthday, her mother told her that she was ashamed of Yu. That's the moment when Yu accepted that her mom was impossible to please. That's when she decided to stop fighting to make her mom proud and start finding worth within herself. Yu's journey of finding self-worth led her to become a role model for the disability community, "My mission is to give other people permission to be themselves."

Despite the constant struggle with her mom, Yu emphasized that her mom—a Taiwanese immigrant, Vietnam refugee, and a single mother who raised four kids while having a job overseas—is a hero. Even though Yu's mother disapproved of her work, the tension did not stop her mom from loving her in her own way. During the COVID-19 pandemic, her mother managed to secure scarce masks and quietly sent Yu boxes of N95 masks.

Yu's impressive story reminds us that we can prevail with a strong conviction in ourselves, despite all the adversity on our path. Yu broke through all the taboo and inspired us to live authentically.

2.

Over 2.9 million Asian Americans were diagnosed with a mental illness in 2020.[79] While model minority did not cause every depression, it is hard to separate the model minority stereotype from our experience. When we do not know others'

---

79 "Asian American/Pacific Islander Communities and Mental Health," Mental Health America, accessed January 19, 2021.

stories, it is easy to dehumanize ourselves and forget we are all humans with similar life struggles.

While the pressures from the model minority stereotype covered our true identities, our families can be another debilitating force. Research from the Centers for Disease Control (CDC) found that one in five high school students has been bullied, and one in seven has been beaten and neglected by a parent in 2020.[80][81] Unfortunately, when I reached out to interview the immigrant parents, everyone declined. I can't help but wonder: What made them give up the power to tell their own stories?

Tess Paras, an actress from *The Crazy Ex-Girlfriend*, recalled her parents saying, "We know you need to go to therapy. We will pay for it, but we are not comfortable talking about it at home."[82] The deafening silence shows that many families are afraid that speaking of pain might traumatize everyone in the family. Altogether, these cultural patterns compromised our mental health. We even have a term—Asian poker face—that describes emotionless Asian men.

It took Grace Chiang four years to begin therapy after her suicidal thoughts surfaced. It took Maggie Yip eight years to receive the medical prescription she needed for her mental health. It took Janet Chang twelve years to realize she

---

80 "Preventing Youth Violence," Centers for Disease Control and Prevention, April 7, 2020.

81 "Preventing Child Abuse & Neglect," Centers for Disease Control and Prevention, April 7, 2020.

82 Stacy Chen, "Asian-American Women Want to End the Stigma around Mental Health Treatment," Good Morning America, September 10, 2018.

experienced abuse as a child. All these stories showed the price we had to pay for our silence, and we are not even counting all the untold stories. Fortunately, Grace, Maggie, and Janet have healed their trauma and become avid mental health advocates for their community.

While their parents may never understand mental health challenges, they care about their children in their own way. "My mom wanted me to be better than her," Maggie told me. "I no longer expected my mom to understand how I felt." As Maggie opened the door to these difficult conversations with her community, she grew to have more compassion and accept her parents as they are.

While the lack of parental support may put us at a disadvantage, we can support each other by healing our community. We have paid too much for neglecting our mental health. We need to start having difficult conversations and help our community today.

3.

Besides the cultural taboo, we could also become the bottleneck of our emotional awareness.

"You scored really high on every area of your life assessment." My life coach Isabel prefaced our new session with this observation.

Of course, I thought to myself. *I mindlessly checked all the boxes to indicate my well-being briefly.*

Isabel was too polite to ask, "Why the hell are you asking for this service?" Instead, she looked at my responses and curiously asked, "What problem would you like to tackle today?"

I didn't prepare an agenda, but my intuition declared, "*Emotion!*"

> **Isabel**: *How do you deal with emotions?*
>
> **Me**: *I don't know. I try to compartmentalize my emotions.*
>
> **Isabel**: *Are you avoiding them?*
>
> **Me**: *What's the difference between avoidance and compartmentalization?*
>
> **Isabel**: *Avoidance is saying that I don't want to feel this because it's too uncomfortable. Compartmentalization is putting the stuff in the closet.*
>
> **Me**: *They sound like the same thing. Perhaps avoidance is a bit more numbing.*
>
> **Isabel**: *That's right.*
>
> **Me**: *How do I tell the difference?*
>
> **Isabel**: *If you are in touch with your emotions, you will know.*

I get annoyed when people go in circles.

4.

I showed up the next week and shared how I coached my mom:

Me: *It was very scary, but very effective…*

Isabel: *That's exciting. Before we proceed, can I get your consent on recording this session?*

Me: *Okay. I was getting ahead of myself. I am feeling something right now.*

Isabel: *Go ahead.*

Me: *I was coaching my mom to love herself and become more assertive, but it scared me to point out that her root cause was her childhood trauma. My husband noticed that my voice was calmer than usual, but I was screaming inside!*

Isabel: *How were you feeling inside your body?*

Me: *I was shaking.*

Isabel: *What else?*

Me: *Frozen, tense, discomfort.*

Isabel: *What are you mostly feeling?*

Me: *Sad.*

I feel like exploding, but somehow my body held it all together. Perhaps my default fight or flight response is suppression. I was sad to hear that my mom almost gave up. I used to believe no one could help people who had already given up.

> **Isabel:** *I can see your sadness when you write these thoughts down.*

It was difficult for me to accept my mom's fear, but I wanted to be there for her. I wanted my mom to be happy. I was sad that her way of living held her back.

The principle of cognitive-behavioral coaching is understanding the connection between thinking and feeling. Once you see the correlation, you can choose to change or defund your thoughts. *Why give resources to limiting beliefs? They are not serving you!*

By getting in touch with my feelings, I spotted my old beliefs. I put many emotions in the closet, afraid that someday they might overflow and collapse.

It took me a while to understand that avoiding emotions wouldn't make the emotions disappear. Avoiding emotions would only prevent me from getting all the information my emotions try to tell me. When I acknowledged my sadness, I was able to stop avoiding my emotions, redirect my energy to focus on what I can control, and find out the important information buried in the unspoken words.

I have included an exercise on accepting your emotion at the end of Chapter Four. Once you embrace your emotions, you no longer need to fight with them anymore.

5.

Ali Wong got a lot of success from embracing sex and shame. She did her first Netflix Special *Baby Cobra* when she was pregnant. In this special, Wong spent twenty-three minutes sharing her miscarriage, fear of giving birth, and the double standards society held toward pregnant ladies.[83] Two years later, she returned with her second Netflix Special *Hard Knock Wife* and spent the first thirty-one minutes talking about her brutal postpartum experiences: "Nobody told me about all the crazy shit that comes out of your pussy after you give birth."

Wong shared her experience of recovering from two C-Sections and breastfeeding her newborn.[84] She was real about all her struggles and the help she got along the way. She powerfully normalized taboos with humor and pride.

When people ask Wong whether her stand-up comedy would isolate her from her parents, she declared proudly and loudly, "My older sister is an unemployed lesbian who lives on my mother's property. So, I can do whatever I want."[85] Wong is the breadwinner in her family and the fearless godmother who has inspired generations of Asians to explore a world of creative possibilities. Her vulnerability and authenticity created great emotional resonance and showed us a way out. That power is contagious.

---

83 *Ali Wong: Baby Cobra*, directed by Jay Karas, written by Ali Wong, featuring Ali Wong, aired May 5, 2016 on Netflix.

84 *Ali Wong: Hard Knock Wife*, directed by Jay Karas, written by Ali Wong, featuring Ali Wong, aired May 13, 2018 on Netflix.

85 Ibid.

While we have role models like Ali Wong, Cathy Park Hong, and Tiffany Yu, we need to do a lot more work within our community.

6.

To heal the people in our community, we can start by cultivating empathy and nurturing deep relationships. This empathy will help us acknowledge their feelings are valid and it's okay to not be okay. You can start by learning the following four attributes of empathy that nursing scholar Theresa Wiseman suggested:

1. See the world as others see it: It requires a deep sense of humility to admit that we don't know what they are experiencing. While it might feel scary, this is actually the best way to close the gap between people.
2. Practice non-judgment: We are just noticing what is happening objectively. We are not asking our loved ones to change. They already know everything. We are here to learn about their truths.
3. Understand their current feelings: Emotion is a muscle. The more we practice it, the more resilient it gets. The best way to understand other people's feelings is to start by opening up our own.
4. Communicate the understanding: Acknowledge their feelings are valid. Let them know you are here for them.[86] As empathy researcher Brené Brown advised, you may say, "I don't know what to say, but I am really glad you told me."[87]

---

86 Theresa Wiseman, "A concept analysis of empathy," Journal of advanced nursing 23.6, 1996, 1162-1167.

87 *RSA*, "Brené Brown on Empathy," December 10, 2013, video, 2:53.

I have turned these four pillars into an empathy exercise:

EXERCISE

STEP 1: GET THEIR PERMISSION TO ASK QUESTIONS.
Once you get their permission, gently ask them how they are feeling.

____

____

____

____

Don't ask if they are okay because we all know that they are not okay. Instead, try to let them explain themselves.

STEP 2: FOLLOW UP WITH A CURIOSITY QUESTION.
Once they express their emotions, ask them, "How would you like to feel?"

____

____

____

____

Acknowledge they know themselves the best. Let them tell you what they would like to feel.

STEP 3: SHARE SOME CONCRETE RESOURCES.

Once they share their ideal state, follow up with, "What are some resources that could be helpful?"

____

____

____

____

This is where you can offer tangible support. For example, "I'm going grocery shopping tomorrow. Want to join me?" or "I am making pasta tonight. Want to come over?" Don't be discouraged if they say no. You are here to show that you care.

The next time you or someone struggles to feel okay, try to practice these frameworks.

What I learned through the process is that helping my friend is also helping me. By nurturing these relationships and helping the community, we can also help ourselves.

PART 3

CHAPTER 9

TO THE NEXT GENERATIONS

Dear Next Generation Leaders,

It might take a while to process your feelings, and that's okay. We are still in the early days.

1.

If there is one common thread among all second- and third-generation Chinese Americans, it has to be the love-hate relationships with Chinese-heritage schools. Although Chinese parents always wanted their children to learn Chinese history, culture, and language, it is hard for kids to take a weekly two-hour Chinese school seriously. First comes the language barrier. Most Chinese Americans are not familiar with their parents' native tongue. Then comes the lack of incentive. Since the teachers are often friendly parents who volunteered in exchange for discounted tuition, they are not always qualified to teach the curriculum. Since the students only see each other once a week, they have little accountability to perform and study well. As my friend Lisa Truong said, "The students and teachers have no incentives to do well. All of us are forced to be here."

Even though some of my friends wanted to skip Chinese School, they acknowledged the importance of seeing people like them. Like my cousin Amelia and my friend Lisa, most kids struggled to see themselves in American education.

It took Lisa fifteen years to reconnect with her true self.

Lisa grew up in Lawrence, Massachusetts. She enjoyed playing in her childhood. But soon after grade school, her free spirit disappeared. As a model student, she followed the rules and had academic success. However, her success came at the expense of her confidence and the courage to dream big. She stopped asking the questions and silenced her curiosity, hoping her compliance would make everyone else's life easier. She rarely looked in the mirror and forgot who she was before becoming the model minority.

Her world changed when she went to Wellesley. She finally saw herself in her Asian American friends, who went through similar struggles of conforming to the culture. She was relieved from being a good girl and began to reinvent herself. She rotated through many majors and friend groups. She learned to ask for help and explore a broader range of cultural perspectives with her Asian American community. She fought back against the stereotype and became proud of her racial identity.

Finally, after fifteen years, she can look in the mirror and say, "I'm beautiful, I'm strong, and I am myself."

Community helps us realize we are not alone. While it might be hard to embrace Chinese Schools, they are a wonderful place to start. This unique experience has provided millions of Chinese Americans the opportunity to build their self-esteem before they get bullied by the white supremacy rooted in our culture.

2.

All of the people I interviewed for this book rejected some parts of themselves during the teenage years.

This struggle is especially prevalent among teenagers who are trying to form their sense of self. On the one hand, they want to fit into their friend groups. On the other hand, they want to make their family proud. They are working so hard to make others happy that they overlook the happiness of themselves. As a result, they felt like an outsider, isolated from everyone. They hated themselves for not feeling more confident about opening up and interacting with new people, but they had always been this way.

When I asked Yuji Lai if she struggled with an identity crisis, she told me she tries not to think about the stereotypes. What she didn't say was that she coped with the model minority stereotype through hard work. This message resonates with high-achieving Chinese students: If you discriminate against me, I'll work hard and be more successful than you, or so-called "success as retribution for racism." But isn't that how the model minority sets up to limit us? How can we outgrow the system that sets up to destroy us? And what would happen when we fail to live up to the increasingly high standards we have set for ourselves?

When my friend Jennifer Li first came to the States at the age of fourteen, she struggled a lot with being the minority at school. While she had a supportive host family, she found it hard to be herself. On the one hand, Jennifer rarely saw people who looked like her in class. On the other hand, she desperately looked to anchor onto something that could concretely help her find out who she was. It was not until college, where she got to meet other smart Asian friends, that she could become more comfortable being Chinese.

While her identity crisis faded as she matured and saw representation in college, she kept a secret from her friends: her real name. She didn't want to be different, so she never shared her Chinese first name with anyone. She had always been known as Jennifer, so she was anxious that the graduation ceremony would "expose" her old identity—one she had quietly held onto and never mentioned to anyone before.

However, a conversation with her mom reminded her she didn't need to be ashamed of anything. When she confessed her concerns, her mom told her, "But that's why you should be proud of yourself. You have traveled so far." The fact that no one knew she grew up in a different country and spoke a foreign language demonstrated her impressive growth. In addition to that, she had the wisdom of American and Chinese cultures and graduated from college. While she always knew she wanted to be Chinese, that conversation had changed her mind and crystallized the moment when she truly, confidently felt that her ethnicity would not limit her anymore.

Sitting with her friends and family in front of Zoom, Jennifer accepted her bachelor's degree with her real name—Changyu Li—on the screen, showing everyone how far she had come. Now that Changyu broke the silence and spoke up for her life, I asked Changyu if she still faced any model minority stereotypes. "When you enter a space where people are more aware of how to respect the multiple identities we have, race and nationality no longer define us," Changyu quipped. "It's their problem. It's not my problem. It's their lack of awareness. I am wonderful."

By embracing everything she has gone through—her Chinese identity and American experiences—Changyu consciously created an empowering and beautiful version of herself. As we gain a new awareness of how others perceive us, we can redefine those stereotypes with what feels true to us. For example, a host family helps force international students like Changyu to see beyond their traditional mindsets and embrace the new culture.

Just like Changyu, we can redefine our relationship with success and embrace who we are.

3.

It turns out that this self-reckoning process is more complicated for Chinese Americans. Chinese Americans often have trouble connecting with their cultural and family values because of the language barrier.

Emily Lin, a master's student at one of the Ivy League schools, found it hard to fully understand what her parents were trying to say. Despite being conversational in Chinese, she still struggled to share her complex emotions and thoughts. If only she spent more time connecting with the Chinese culture, she could understand how her parents think. As elaborated in Chapter Four, to heal our relationship with our parents, we need to heal the relationship with ourselves.

Emily told me she felt begrudgingly toward Chinese culture growing up. Her cultural identity made her stand out in her white neighborhood in New York and attracted bullies. She was bullied into wishing she could be white. It was not until middle school, when she got to see role models among Korean pop stars and Asian YouTubers, that she came to appreciate her identity more. Coincidently, the kids who had bullied her before no longer made fun of her anymore.

While Korean pop stars and Asian YouTubers may seem like pure entertainment, they also serve as role models to many people who struggle to be themselves. They show the world we could be just as complicated, full of life, and human as everyone else. They show us our stories matter.

Lisa reconnected with herself after bonding with her community at Wellesley. Changyu found a new version of herself through the encouragement of her mom. Emily discovered who she wanted to be through following her role models.

Representation matters.

4.

Once we realize the power of our stories, we need to face the most common cause of bullying: racism.

Most of my interviewees had experienced racism in some form. Some were microaggressions that were assumed in everyday conversation. Others were intentional bullying that eroded their sense of self and identity. Thus, it might not be surprising to see that 15 percent of Asian Americans reported having a mental illness in the past year, let alone the ones who struggle to speak up.[88] These anti-Asian sentiments led to the rising anxiety and fear lashed out against Chinese people, as referenced in Chapter Three.

The Chinese kids in a white classroom have two terrible options: They could either fit into the mold or get bullied. They may stand up and bear the risk of a decade-long emotional trauma, or they may protect themselves by being silent and fitting into the model minority. After all, the bully wanted to trick you into believing that you were inferior and had no power to fight back.

In that office hour when the alumni mentor silenced me, I didn't speak up for myself and let the stereotype define me. It took me years to realize that I wasn't the one who needed to be sorry. If one instance was already that damaging, how much more damage would it do to the youth growing up through these bullies while their sense of self was even less solidified?

---

88 "Asian American/Pacific Islander Communities and Mental Health," Mental Health America, accessed January 19, 2021.

We need to realize that the authority may not always be right, so you need to think for yourself. With our new story, we can confront people who force their worldviews upon us and break the stereotypes effectively.

I'm no longer intimidated by the challenges. We are stronger than we think. Let's speak up for each other.

CHAPTER 10

TO THE YOUNG PROFESSIONALS

Dear Young Professionals,

While statistics might disfavor your talents and potential, don't forget that millions of people are rooting for your success.

1.

Yul Kwon represents the new face of the model minority. He had all the credentials we expected of high-achievers—Stanford undergraduate, Yale Law School, Google executive—yet he did a lot more than that. He attended Officer Candidates School for the Marine Corps, taught at the FBI Academy, and won the thirteenth season of the CBS reality show, *Survivor.* What most people don't know, however, is that Yul struggled with crippling social anxiety issues that dominated his life and shaped who he is today.

As a child, Yul had a lisp and was bullied for being the quiet Asian boy in the room. While he struggled socially, he desperately wanted to be normal. Out of desperation, he began to push himself out of his comfort zone little by little. He eventually began putting himself in uncomfortable situations that he knew would force him to adapt, such as signing up for a drama class and joining sports teams to find the support system he couldn't find naturally.

During college, he applied for and was accepted into the Marines Corps' Officer Candidates School, which is known as being one of the hardest "boot camps" in the military. "It was both the worst and best experience in my life till then," Yul said. Halfway through the program, he was ranked last in his platoon by his fellow candidates, who thought he was "too nice." Both they and his instructors criticized him for lacking discipline, not understanding that his passive posture and tone of voice was the result of his cultural upbringing: Be quiet and submissive to your social superiors. That experience made him realize how people would interpret his behavior based on lack of context and false assumptions—a lesson he took to heart and internalized by changing his own behavior to match the social environment.

Ten years after college, he got a call to join the final round of *Survivor.* "The reason they wanted to do this was that they had a twist to that season," Yul shared on the *NPR* podcast, "which was they were going to divide the contestants into racial tribes and have a war of races."[89] While he was dis-

89 NPR Staff, "Yul Kwon, From Bullying Target to Reality TV Star," NPR, May 15, 2012.

turbed by how he was tokenized, he desperately wanted to increase Asian American representation in the media. More importantly, he was excited to be himself, not reading off any script. He wanted to become the role model he never had. "If I can get through this, I can do anything."

After Yul became the first Asian American to win *Survivor* on the Cook Islands, he broke the bamboo ceiling in the Silicon Valley. Bamboo ceiling, first coined by executive coach and author Jane Hyun, is used to describe Asian Americans' lack of leadership representation in the corporate world.[90] Yul also noticed a significant drop-off from entry-level to senior leadership among Asian colleagues. He realized that part of this gap came from the stereotype that Asians are smart and hardworking but lack strong leadership or communication skills. Cognizant of this stereotype and the possibility of implicit bias, he intentionally learned to communicate in ways more aligned with how leaders in corporate environments are expected to communicate—for example, by speaking in a deeper tone and slowing down his speech.

Yul's cognizant social perceptions enabled him to rise through the ranks and take on greater leadership roles over the course of his career. This raises the question, however, of whether adopting behaviors required to overcome the model minority myth necessarily comes at the cost of "selling out" and abandoning your Asian identity for an Americanized one. In Yul's experience, some level of behavioral conformity is often necessary before a person can reach a position of influence from

---

90 Jane Hyun, *Breaking the Bamboo Ceiling: Career Strategies for Asians* (New York: Harper Business, 2006), Kindle.

which they can effectively advocate for systemic change and mentor other members of their community. But that doesn't mean the person is selling out—a person can superficially adjust their outward behavior to be successful in a given environment while staying true to their internal values and cultural identity.

On the difference between conforming just enough and selling out, I think the key difference lies in whether we are honoring who we are. If we conform too much, we will be restricted by the rules and have no impact. If we conform too little, we will be seen as an outsider and get expelled by the community. The key is to conform just enough so that you could have the impact you want. Like Yul, following the dominant expectations and speaking the language may help people hear you more. As we develop self-awareness and understand our boundaries, we can be strategic about how much we conform. While I deeply admire all the achievements of Yul, another part of me can't help but wonder, *Do we always have to minimize our identities and experiences? Is there a way to be seen and accepted as ourselves?*

As a leader, Yul has lent his privilege and platform by sharing his story with us here. There is no right or wrong way to break the model minority stereotype. In an ideal world, we can honor our values, tell our own story, and be proud of who we are. Sometimes the system would get in our way. Sometimes we are inclined to fit in. Sometimes we may have no choice. If compromising makes you productive, it could certainly be your short-term coping strategy. It all depends on your comfort level. The hope is that eventually, you will get the leverage of talent and have the privilege to take it to somewhere that celebrates who you are.

2.

Research shows that Yul is not alone in experiencing these struggles.

As successful as Yul is, he still experiences imposter syndrome. Despite the progress made over the years, very few Asians made it to leadership positions like Yul did. A Harvard Business Review study showed that even though Asians are the most likely to be hired into high-tech jobs, Asian Americans are the least likely racial group to be promoted to management and executive positions.[91] Such disparity between the promotion from entry-level to the executive level suggests that Asian Americans either lack some core leadership traits or key sponsorships to climb through the ranks. The former indicates that they are inferior, or perceived less than other racial groups, which is ridiculous and racist. The latter suggests that we need to coach potential Asian leaders to close the jarring diversity gap.

Furthermore, we are the silent minority in a company's diversity report. In Intel's 2019 Diversity Report, Asian males are

91 The analysis of national EEOC workforce data shows that White professionals are about twice as likely to be promoted into management as their Asian American counterparts. The findings might be even more jarring when we see that Asian Americans are the most highly educated racial group with the highest median income. Buck Gee and Denise Peck, "Asian Americans Are the Least Likely Group in the US to Be Promoted to Management," Harvard Business Review, May 31, 2018.

grouped under the majority population and Asian females are grouped under females.[92] On the other hand, Hispanic, African American, and Native Americans all have their separate racial category. If we are not even represented in a company's diversity report, how are we going to be seen?

To address these systematic stereotypes, companies also need to institutionalize the objective to increase Asian American leadership with clear objectives and accountability. Without the numbers to back it up, the inclusion program could only give us the illusion that things are getting better, while most people are staring at the headlines and wondering why life hasn't changed much.

3.

The pattern of adapting the Western cultural expectation is not unique to Yul. Helen Bui, a seasoned media executive from *News Corp* and the *Wall Street Journal* (*WSJ*), told me about the importance of self-confidence and promotion. When she first started her corporate job at *WSJ*, she carried the immigrant mentality to quietly work hard. Before long, she noticed her less hardworking white colleagues were getting the promotions she thought she deserved. She was devastated and decided to change her mindset.

"When we are too focused on putting our heads down and working hard toward success, we will have no time for

92 "Asian American Executive Program," Stanford Graduate School of Business, 2020.

ourselves," Helen told me. "As I began to find my voice and promote myself, I began to garner respect."

Growing up, she was often told what she should be, so it took the extra effort to find herself. As she found her voice and spoke up for herself, she was able to understand the stereotype to better meet her own goals and desires. She defied the stereotype that Asian women were meek, did not ask for more or take on risky projects, and smashed the bamboo ceiling.

By speaking up and pushing back, Helen was able to show what others had not expected to see from her—a strong and extremely competent leader. Helen was promoted to manage the profits and losses for *Wall Street Journal* and became the first Asian and person of color executive to reach such a high position in the company. Ironically, Helen only got strong mentorship after—not before—she made it. "Executives don't mentor folks who just work hard," she noticed. "They mentor folks who demonstrate 'leadership potential,' which Asians are often perceived to lack." These executive mentorships are critical to growing leaders, but they often came too late in our careers.

4.

"Cut your upspeak." Professor Barbara Tannenbaum would stomp her feet whenever someone ended a sentence in a rising intonation in our public speaking classes. Rising intonation would make us sound unsure of ourselves. I learned ways to be perceived better. I was amazed by how these slight behavioral changes would shift the way others perceive us. It is ultimately up to you to decide whether you want to compromise or be compromised.

Sharon Chen, a former founder who went through the Y Combinator program, told me she didn't have much success raising investor money when she dressed casually.[93] Frustrated, she changed her dress code and began to wear pants, heels, and leather jackets, clothes that projected confidence and assertiveness. After that outfit change, she began to raise more money. Sharon's strategy is validated by the researchers in the *Journal of Experimental Psychology*, who found that male participants who dressed up were perceived to be more successful and receive more profitable deals.[94] While the adjustments have been financially rewarding, I was afraid we might lose sight of who we are and empower the current system.

5.

Many senior leaders in the Silicon Valley credit their career growth to the support from their leadership. I was told by a few mentors that Asians need more visibility and stretched opportunities to make ourselves seen. The Harvard Business Review study also found that companies with strong CEOs and executive support were able to quickly identify Asian leaders and shift their leadership priorities. Such open support is critical to change the legacy systems and allocate

---

93 I've changed their name and identifying details.

94 Wendy Berry Mendes, "Sartorial symbols of social class elicit class-consistent behavioral and physiological responses: A dyadic approach," *Journal of Experimental Psychology: General*, *143*(6), 2330–2340.

budget for leadership training. For example, Stanford Graduate School of Business has created an Asian-American Executive Program to help managers bridge the cultural gap with its leadership development curriculum.[95] While these leadership programs teach us how to live up to the dominant culture's expectations and succeed in the current systems, they are only short-term solutions. They are not breaking the stereotypes.

Some have criticized cultural and behavioral enrichment programs, claiming that they enforce cultural assimilation and impose cultural superiority. However, these programs also help us understand the best practices to succeed. We can learn a lot about the power structure and unspoken rules, which are often so subtle that outsiders cannot even see them. With this new awareness, we can influence and change the cultural narrative more effectively.

6.

Changes start from awareness. It is challenging to change the culture on our own, so we need sponsors and allies to advocate for the change. While internal organizations set out to promote cultural inclusion, leaders also need to get educated. We need to help them get rid of biases like "Asians follow orders, work hard, and stay quiet." While not every corporation is open to talking about this "taboo" topic, here are some concrete frameworks to help you assert influence at work while being yourself:

95 "2019 Annual Intel Diversity and Inclusion Report," Intel, 2019.

EXERCISE

PROMOTE YOUR STRENGTHS

What are you most proud of? Write out how you accomplished the wins or overcame the hurdles.

Like Helen, you can help people understand the hard work you have done. By highlighting the facts and the impact you made happen, you can build your influence without bragging too much.

Reflect on the most recent question you got at work. How did you answer the question?

When people ask you questions such as, "How long will it take you to run the experiment?" Your first response may be "Three weeks." However, this type of prevention question focuses on potential risks and your responsibility. On the other hand, promotion questions focus on potential gains and your upward trajectory. Laura Huang and her colleague found that entrepreneurs who were asked promotion questions raised seven times more than those who were asked prevention questions.[96]

Once you answer the prevention question quickly, shift the focus to a promotion question.

____

____

____

____

Once you answer, "How long will it take you to run the experiment?" turn the focus to "How you plan to make the launch successful." By effectively reframing the focus, you can shift people's attention from your weaknesses to strengths.

96 Dana Kanze et al., "Male and Female Entrepreneurs Get Asked Different Questions by VCs — and It Affects How Much Funding They Get," *Harvard Business Review*, June 27, 2017.

EXERCISE

FIND YOUR SPONSORS

Sponsors are the key people who will stand up for you and recommend you when the opportunity comes.

How can you create rapport with your leadership team?

____

____

____

____

For example, I volunteered to take notes in executive strategy sessions. This enabled me to see what they cared about and how I could frame the message in a way that can be better received.

Seek feedback from your potential sponsor. How can you ask hard questions?

____

____

____

____

Lead with service. If you consistently deliver great work, but sense that your manager is not your sponsor yet, consider asking them, "I want to take on a stretch assignment to grow more. What can I do to create the most impact?"

Feedback is a gift. How can you act on their feedback and follow up?

____

____

____

____

While it might be hard to understand why someone is not yet sponsoring you, you can learn a lot from their candid feedback. Be willing to propose changes accordingly: "These are the five things that I really want to work on...." Share how their feedback changed your actions and point of view.

How can you invest in relationships for the long term?

____

____

____

____

Follow up with concrete actions to address the challenges. Be vulnerable and open.

By doing the work and showing your progress, you will be surprised to learn that sponsors and mentors often get as much as you do through the process.

As we continue to promote our strengths and grow from mentors, we can close the gap between entry-level and senior leaders among Asians.

CONCLUSION

1.

When I was a child, I loved to read the children's book series *I Wonder Why*. I always had more questions than answers, and I demanded my younger brother Warren answer my questions. I wondered why parents would harm their own children. I wondered why my best friends could never be happy. I wondered why so many people wanted to be someone other than themselves.

Even though Warren replied with more questions than answers, his response started our lifelong conversations and inspired me to write a *Dear Warren* series on my blog. I wrote about my college and life experience in America. While Warren only responded to one letter, more than 50,000 visitors have read about it. I even met another Warren Wang who reached out on LinkedIn to learn more.

As I write the final words of *Model Breakers*, I have extended the childhood wonders into multiple shades of the immigrant story. The questions that I asked in this book are not much different from the ones I asked as a child. Through my research and interview, I understood why many people struggled to be fully themselves.

When I interviewed Warren for this book, I was surprised to learn that my quiet brother was so comfortable and confident about himself. "My intuition helped me stay calm under the most stressful situations," Warren recalled the time when he was competing for the International Physics Olympiad. "I am satisfied about what I have achieved." I also learned that the question, "Have I done enough?" has guided him to take up new challenges and create his own meaning of life. "I don't let others' problems get to me," Warren shrugged at the model minority stereotype. After all, he has achieved what many thought was impossible—won the Physics Olympiad Gold Medal and transferred from National Taiwan University to MIT.

I didn't want him to lose these qualities when he came to America.

2.

Despite being quiet, Warren is watching the world. He watches the news and forms his own opinions. While he may not be the first one to fight back unfair treatments, he will pick the fight when his right is invaded.

Warren's sentiment is shared among the Chinese community, which may explain why most Chinese are not engaging in American politics or sharing their stories. This silence begs the question: Where do we stand in the society?

Through this book, I tapped into my professional experience and my personal journey from the shy girl to discovering my own voice.

Now I want to leave you with a fun homework assignment: Share your story.

Why are we not organized to speak or fundraise for the causes that matter to us? Despite systemic racism, most of the harm is reinforced by the rest of us who are quiet and have no intention to harm ourselves. Fortunately, we can break this vicious cycle by sharing our stories.

Bryan Pham, founder of Asian Hustle Network, has influenced the Asian community through storytelling. Bryan has created a 70,000-people community where everyone comes to share their successes and resources. Bryan told me, "It takes a lot for us to be open and willing to share resources, but once we open the floodgate, Asian people will be the ones to pull you up as well." By scrolling through authentic stories, community members can get past the competition mindset and embrace the abundance mindset that we can help each other to succeed together.

You can start by:

- reviewing the action steps at the end of Chapter Six.
- learning more about your parents' stories.
- sharing your past experiences with close friends.
- interviewing Asian leaders and sharing how they overcome their challenges.

- highlighting the awesome work of Asian owned businesses and charities.

- sharing on social media and tagging #ModelBreakers to get a special shoutout.

By sharing our stories, we can redefine the stereotypes, embrace our authentic selves, and invite our community to do the same.

3.

After thousands of hours of interviews and research, I realized that many people, like Warren, are just waiting for the right time to speak up and tell their own story. However, we have already seen too many microaggressions and bullies targeted to our community. There is no better time than now.

It is time to be a model breaker. It is time to speak up. The process is going to be messy. I have laid out some options to get you started in a promising direction. The process may stretch us out of our comfort zone, but the effort would further everyone's success. If you would like to get more resources on how to get started, I would like to invite you to join the LivingOS Community at LivingOS.org. It is the biggest gift I've given to my community, and I would love to help you embark on your own journey.

Challenge the beliefs that keep us quiet. Appeal the rules that limit your dream. Share the ideas that you were too afraid to say out loud. Speak up for the community. These actions are all going to help us become better.

Let's break the model minority together.

RECOMMENDED RESOURCES

Thank you so much for taking the time to read this book.

Here are a few resources to help you jump start your journey as a model breaker:

1. **Bonus Materials:** If you enjoyed the ideas in this book, you may wonder how you can apply the lessons to your life. I curated a list of books, support groups, practical guides, and more to help you if you struggle with any of the issues we discussed in this book. You can download at: livingos.org/breakers.

2. **Weekly Newsletter:** If you enjoyed this book, you may like my latest writings too. I share my latest projects, inspirations, and coaching conversations in a weekly newsletter. You can sign up at: livingos.org/newsletter.

3. **Lifelong Community:** If you would like to join the conversation and get ongoing support, you can share your experiences on social media with #ModelBreakers or join the LivingOS Community at livingos.org/fellowship.

Thank you for going on this adventure with me.

ACKNOWLEDGMENTS

It took me two weeks to write this acknowledgment because this book is truly a team effort. I am deeply grateful to the many people who believed in these ideas and made the publication of *Model Breakers* possible.

My deepest thanks go to my writing coach, Chris Liu. Chris and I have been working together on hundreds of newsletters and later this book. He put in late nights, weekends, and holidays to accommodate the schedule of my intuition. Chris's talent with structure gently held up my ideas. He coached me to rewrite each chapter with effective outlines, interview his amazing friends, and rewrite each story with my authentic voice. His intelligence and diligence made the book a lot more rigorous and insightful. Not only has he made this book possible, but he also became my partner in life. Thank you for showering me with unconditional love and inspiring me to become better versions of myself. I love you more than words can express.

To my wonderful team at LivingOS: Thank you for trusting me when I spoke and listening to my stories. Each of you fills my heart with love and my mind with wisdom every day. I can't mention LivingOS without my amazing team: Ju-Han Tarn, Eva Huang, and Sherry Hsiao, and the hundreds of people who shared their stories as fellows and special guests: Stefanie Yu Molina, Julia Xu, Christina Qi, Grace Chiang, Angie Zhu, Kimmie Chin, Susie Li, Anya Cheng, Cat Chen, Mary Yuan, Joyce Bao, Janice Lai, Ben Hart, Anthony McGuire, Lisa Truong, Alexander Sam, Connie Truong, Kunzhao Li, Zhaoyi Zhang, Olivia Chun, Jen-Feng Chang, Cara Jefferson, Alice Chen, Renee Huang, Meghana Subramaniam, Max Zhang, Charles Chen, Viola Chiu, Tzu-Ying Wu, Ashley Lin, Nicole Chui, Yung-Chen Chen, and many more lovely fellows to come. When I needed inspiration, I would watch your talks and read your letters many times.

To my compassionate leadership coaches: Charlie, Isabelle, and Marjoire, thank you for seeing the potential in me and supporting me to become a better leader. I will continue to bring my inquisitive mind and lean into your wisdom. I love each of you.

I'm grateful to my friend Haley Hoffman Smith, who introduced me to Eric Koester and the entire team at New Degree Press. I want to thank Chelsea Olivia and Whitney Jones in particular—your insightful editing and incredible resources have made this book a pleasure to write. I really appreciate the work you do.

This book would not exist without the Model Breakers who generously shared their stories. Special thanks to my brother Warren Wang, my cousin Amelia and Isabelle Zai, Janet Chang, Grace Chiang, Lisa Truong, Cissy Hu, Murong Xu, Candice Lee, Emily Lin, Yuji Lai, Changyu Li, Amy Deng, Kelly Wang, Anthony Chen, Maggie Yip, Kristen Fang, Tiffany

Yu, Bryan Pham, Siqi Mou, Helen Bui, and Yul Kwon, and the dozens who preferred to remain anonymous. Your stories and lessons are the essence of this book. *Model Breakers* will touch so many lives.

Deep gratitude and sincere thanks to my amazing community at On Deck: Natalie Toren, Reza Saeedi, Tom White, Justin Norman, Federico Antoni, Matt Knight, Will Quist, Mohammed Malik, Nicholas Sclafani, Benjamin Strak, Caroline Nguyen, Kevin Lee, Racha Ghamlouch, Rahim Adatia, Sara Grover, Saya Iwasaki, Girish Gupta, Sasha Levage, Alicia Kenworthy, Robbie Crabtree, and more. You have each taught me how to become a better writer. Thank you all for your generous contributions.

Halfway through this journey, I shared an early version of *Model Breakers* online with my campaign backers. Hundreds of early readers reviewed it. They debated, shared research, and edited the words themselves. Thousands of comments honed this book. I owe particular gratitude to my dear author community, particularly Ashley Chen and Chung-Hsin Hsu, whose keen minds transformed this book. Thank you all.

Thanks to all the teachers, mentors, and authors whose work have inspired me to discover my own journey of *Model Breakers*. I am forever indebted: Mr. Yang, Julice Chen, Richard M. Locke, James Morone, Howard Anderson, Jerry Colonna, Alex Linde, Khanh Nguyen, Debbie Ferguson, Laura Huang, Deborah Liu, Kevin Zhang, Neel Mehta, Anne Kerkian, Pei-Ping Lin, Chelsea Fischbach, Allan McNichol, and so many more.

Thanks to all of you that I still have not yet met but will break through the stereotypes and rewrite your narratives.

Thank you to the individuals that supported my pre-launch campaign:

Akshay Tilak
Alan Lin
Alan Liu
Alon Galor
Alyssa Pho
Amy Wang
Anand Mariappan
Andy Jhong-Yi Hsu
Antony Ting
Arjun Lalwani
Atira Richards
Benjamin Jen
Bernard Liang
Brian Cheung
Carolyn Skowron
Celine Chen
Charles Shao
Charmaine Hung
Chen Shan-Chih
Cheng Ching hau
ChienYi Sunny Wang
Christina Ma
Christine Z. Chapman
Chu Cheng Long
Chun Chou Lin
Chung-Hsi Lai
Cindy Lin
Cissy Hu
Claire Jacobson
Cristian Cibils
Darsh Thakkar
David Chen
David Fontenot
David Lu
Derek Li
Dominika Kamola
Elaine Kao
Emily Liu
Erica Lin
Erin Bugbee
Evelyn Lee
Fan Zhang
Feng Shen
Gary Zhou
Gigi Leung
Grace Cheng
Gurinder Singh
Hank Chung
Hao Tong
Hengliang Zhang
Henry Wu
Hiroyuki Kuwana
Hsiangping Huang
Hui Tzu Lee
Isabella Teng
Ivy Liang
Jady Tsao
Jamie Lin
Jamie Zhang

Jane Y
Janice Yang
Jeannette Goon
Jessica Zhu
Jessie Jiang
Jia Zhuo
Jieqi Kang
Jing Wang
Jingyuan Wu
Jinshan Jia
Jintao Xuan
Joanna Hoang
Joanna Tasmin
Joe Liu
Jordan Shaw
Judy Shum
Judy Wang
Julia Wu
June Jo Lee
Junfei Huang
Karen Kim
Ken Cheng
Kevin King
Kinton Cheung
Ko Ko Lwin
Kun Huang
Kushaan Shah
Leo Li
Liang-yu Peng
Lilu Xu
Lily Li
Lisa HN
Liuyi Zhu
Luke Skywalker
Manish Arora
Margaret Zai
Marshall Lerner
Mary Weber
Mary Yuan
Matt Susskind
May Chang
Meryam Bukhari
Michelle Kim
Michelle Ma
Naiwen Hu
Nancy Farah
Parker Merritt
Parthi Loganathan
Peggy Chen
Pengquan Meng
Pranav Mutatkar
Qiuxuan Wu
Rajiv Kapoor
Resa Chen
Roger Farley
Rohan Kohli
Ruhan Dong
Ruyi Chiang
Shang-Yi Yu
Sharlene Chen
Sharon Chang
Sharon Lo
Shishi Fu
Shunyao Li
Simone Brathwaite
Siyu Chen
Sophia Cheng
Tamara Scott
Tania Wu

Tessa Eng
Tianren Dong
Tiffany Perumpail
Tina Tuan
Ting-Wei Chiang
Trung Vu
Tsung-Han Yang
Tyson Mao
Tzu Hsin Lin
Tzung De Wang
Vincent Po
Wen Fei Su
Xe Chang
Xiaocong Liang
Xiaoyi Sheng
Xiaoyu Chen
Yang Feng-Jung
Yen Ru Chi
Yen Ru Chi
Yi Wu
Yi-Hsuan Lee
Yike Li
YiXiang Lin
You-Yi Jau
Yu-Chan Chien
Yu-Hui Huang
Yuanru Qian
Yuchen Dai
Yuzhou Jia
Zhe Li
Zhifan Li
Zhihui Xie
Zhirong Liang

I am lucky to work every day with brilliant minds at Google, especially my guardian angels Carlos Façanha and Maciej Michalski. So much of what I am able to do is because of their trust, leadership, and empowerment.

I'm sure there are people I have forgotten, but I keep an updated list of anyone who has influenced my thinking in meaningful ways at livingos.org/thanks.

And finally, this book is dedicated to my family: Mom, thank you for watching me take every fearless step and reassuring me that the sky is my limit. Dad, thank you for sharing my work and inspiring me to strive for excellence at all times. Warren, thank you for giving me a reason to write this book. I knew you would be the first one to read the book.

NOTES

INTRODUCTION

Karas, Jay, dir. *Ali Wong: Baby Cobra*. Aired May 5, 2016, on Netflix. https://www.netflix.com/title/80101493.

Kim, Laura, ed. "Confronting Asian-American Stereotypes." *The New York Times*, June 23, 2018. https://www.nytimes.com/2018/06/23/us/confronting-asian-american-stereotypes.html.

Wong, Ali. *Dear Girls: Intimate Tales, Untold Secrets & Advice for Living Your Best Life*. New York: Penguin Press, 2016. Kindle.

Thai, Ted. 1987. "TIME Magazine Cover: Asian-American Whiz Kids." *Time*, August 31, 1987. http://content.time.com/time/covers/0,16641,19870831,00.html.

CHAPTER ONE: HISTORY OF CHINESE AS "MODEL MINORITY"

Apri Park. ""Honey Nut Cheerios" - a Poem about Growing up Asian-American."April 8, 2019. Video, 2:55. https://youtu.be/ybJoJsLxuD8.

Chan, Melissa. "Photo of Scarlett Johansson in Ghost in the Shell Reignites 'Whitewashing' Controversy." *Time*, April 18, 2016. https://time.com/4297950/scarlett-johansson-ghost-shell-whitewashing/.

Ellis, Mark R. "Denver's Anti-Chinese Riot." Encyclopedia of the Great Plains. Accessed January 4, 2021. http://plainshumanities.unl.edu/encyclopedia/doc/egp.asam.011.

Guo, Jeff. "The Real Reasons the US Became Less Racist toward Asian Americans." *The Washington Post*, April 29, 2019. https://www.washingtonpost.com/news/wonk/wp/2016/11/29/the-real-reason-americans-stopped-spitting-on-asian-americans-and-started-praising-them/.

History.com Editors. "Tiananmen Square Protests," May 31, 2019. https://www.history.com/topics/china/tiananmen-square.

History.com Staff. "Chinese Exclusion Act." HISTORY. A&E Television Networks, August 24, 2018. https://www.history.com/topics/immigration/chinese-exclusion-act-1882.

Hong, Cathy Park. *Minor Feelings: An Asian American Reckoning.* New York: One World, 2020. Kindle.

"Model Minority Section." Stereotypes, Identity, and Belonging Lab (SIBL) at the University of Washington (2011). https://depts.washington.edu/sibl/Publications/Model%20Minority%20Section%20(2011).pdf

Ramakrishnan, Karthick. "The Asian American Vote in 2016: Record Gains, but Also Gaps." Data Bits, May 19, 2017. http://aapidata.com/blog/voting-gains-gaps/.

Rogers, Katie, Lara Jakes, and Ana Swanson. "Trump Defends Using 'Chinese Virus' Label, Ignoring Growing Criticism." *The New York Times*, March 18, 2020. https://www.nytimes.com/2020/03/18/us/politics/china-virus.html.

Sayej, Nadja. "'Forgotten by Society' – How Chinese MIGRANTS Built the Transcontinental Railroad," July 18, 2019. https://www.theguardian.com/artanddesign/2019/jul/18/forgotten-by-society-how-chinese-migrants-built-the-transcontinental-railroad.

Sharma, Prageeta. "A Situation for Mrs. Biswas." Academy of American Poets, 2010. https://poets.org/poem/situation-mrs-biswas.

"Thirty-Seventh Congress, Sess. II, Ch. 25, 27 1862." Accessed January 4, 2021. http://legisworks.org/sal/12/stats/STATUTE-12-Pg340.pdf (site discontinued).

CHAPTER TWO: REDEFINE THE STEREOTYPES

Dweck, Carol. *Mindset: The New Psychology of Success.* New York: Ballantine Books, 2007.

Huang, Laura. *Edge: Turning Adversity Into Advantage.* New York: Penguin, 2020.

Kahneman, Daniel. *Thinking, Fast and Slow.* New York: Farrar, Straus and Giroux, 2011.

Staff Writer. "Five Things You Should Know about Trigeminal Neuralgia." MHealth.org, July 27, 2016. https://www.mhealth.org/blog/2016/july-2016/five-things-you-should-know-about-trigeminal-neuralgia.

Yang, Wesley. "What Happens to All the Asian-American Overachievers When the Test-Taking Ends?" *New York Magazine*, May 6, 2011. https://nymag.com/news/features/asian-americans-2011-5/.

CHAPTER THREE: WHY IT'S IMPORTANT FOR CHINESE AMERICANS TO BREAK THE MODEL NOW

ABC News. "Doctor dragged off United Airlines flight says he 'cried' watching the video." April 9, 2019. Video, 4:04.
https://youtu.be/_anhvdWf3DM.

Capatides, Christina. "Bullies Attack Asian American Teen at School, Accusing Him of Having Coronavirus." *CBS News*, February 14, 2020.
https://www.cbsnews.com/news/coronavirus-bullies-attack-asian-teen-los-angeles-accusing-him-of-having-coronavirus/.

Chao, Claire, and Isabel Sun Chao. *Remembering Shanghai: A Memoir of Socialites, Scholars and Scoundrels*. Plum Brook, 2018. Kindle.

Coates, Ta-Nehisi. *Between the World and Me*. New York: Spiegel & Grau, 2015. Kindle.

Dao, David. *Dragged Off: Refusing to Give Up My Seat on the Way to the American Dream*. Florida: Mango, 2021. Kindle.
https://www.amazon.com/Dragged-Off-Refusing-American-Dream/dp/1642504017/.

Hartocollis, Anemona. "Harvard Rated Asian-American Applicants Lower on Personality Traits, Suit Says." *The New York Times*, June 15, 2018.
https://www.nytimes.com/2018/06/15/us/harvard-asian-enrollment-applicants.html.

Ho, Elizabeth (@RealElizabethHo). 2020. "Yo. So the other day I was in an elevator and I used my elbow to touch a button. Old dude says "oh. Coronavirus?" And I was like "don't have it but trying to be prepared." Twitter, March 12, 2020. 8:21 p.m.
https://twitter.com/RealElizabethHo/status/1238304263467446272.

Cruz, Megan Dela, Danielle Chan, Emerson Min, Gracie Veiga, Joanne Lee, Katie Lin, and Natalie Chen, *et al*. "They Blamed Me Because I am Asian: Findings from Youth-Reported Incidents of AntiAAPI Hate." Stop AAPI Hate. Accessed January 3, 2021.
https://stopaapihate.org/wp-content/uploads/2020/09/Stop-AAPI-Hate-Youth-Campaign-Report-9-17.pdf

Inside Edition. "Doctor Was On Phone With United Moments Before Being Dragged Off Plane." April 12, 2017. Video, 2:49.
https://youtu.be/Dk2Y_VL5e7s.

Lee, Jasmine C., Annie Daniel, Rebecca Lieberman, Blacki Migliozzi, Alexander Burns, and Sarah Almukhtar. "Which Democrats Are Leading the 2020 Presidential Race?" *The New York Times*, June 14, 2019.
https://www.nytimes.com/interactive/2020/us/elections/democratic-polls.html.

Moore, Tina, and Olivia Bensimon. "Asian Man Spat on in Latest Coronavirus Hate Crime in Brooklyn Station." *New York Post*, March 25, 2020.
https://nypost.com/2020/03/25/asian-man-spat-on-in-latest-coronavirus-hate-crime-in-brooklyn-station/.

Palmer, Ewan. "Asian Woman Allegedly Attacked in New York Subway Station for Wearing Protective Mask." *Newsweek*, February 5, 2020.
https://www.newsweek.com/new-york-subway-attack-coronavirus-woman-mask-1485842.

Powell, Jason. "I Was on United Flight 3411. Here's What I Saw." *Chicago Tribune*, May 10, 2019.
https://www.chicagotribune.com/opinion/letters/ct-united-flight-3411-man-dragged-witness-20170411-story.html.

Samson, Carl. "89-Year-Old Chinese American Woman Set on Fire in NYC." *NextShark*, July 27, 2020.
https://nextshark.com/fire-89-year-old-chinese-american-woman-nyc.

Samson, Carl. "Chinese Man's Teeth Knocked Out, Suffers Brain Hemorrhage After Random Attack in NYC." *NextShark*, February 23, 2021.
https://nextshark.com/chinese-man-beaten-anti-asian-attack-new-york/.

Victor, Daniel, and Matt Stevens. "United Airlines Passenger Is Dragged From an Overbooked Flight." *The New York Times*, April 10, 2017.
https://www.nytimes.com/2017/04/10/business/united-flight-passenger-dragged.html.

CHAPTER FOUR: KNOW YOURSELF

ABCs Of Attraction | JT Tran's Dating Advice & PUA Bootcamps for Asian Men. "Jerry 'JT' Tran at Yale University about Asian American Dating (Part 9)." July 26, 2011. Video, 7:01.
https://youtu.be/h7elmo7EBK8.

Chiang, Grace. "Healing the Whole Family." *The New York Times*, September 22, 2020.
https://www.nytimes.com/2020/09/22/well/family/childhood-trauma-family.html.

Chun, Jed. "A Reflection on Asian Intergenerational Trauma." Asian Mental Health Collective. Asian Mental Health Collective, November 1, 2019.
https://www.asianmhc.org/community/a-reflection-on-asian-intergenerational-truama.

E.E. Werner and R.S. Smith, *Overcoming the Odds: High Risk Children from Birth to Adulthood* (Ithaca, NY, and London: Cornell University Press, 1992).

Manson, Mark. *The Subtle Art of Not Giving a F*ck.* San Francisco: HarperOne, 2016. Kindle.

Thompson, Matt. "Five Reasons Why People Code-Switch." *NPR*, April 13, 2013.
https://www.npr.org/sections/codeswitch/2013/04/13/177126294/five-reasons-why-people-code-switch.

Tsai, Jeanne L. "Ideal Affect: Cultural Causes and Behavioral Consequences." Perspectives on Psychological Science 2, 2007. 242–59.

van der Kolk, Bessel. *The Body Keeps the Score: Brain, Mind, and Body in the Healing of Trauma*. United States, New York: Penguin Publishing Group, 2015.

Wang, Charlene and Juhan. "Issue #61 - Talk Show Spotlight - Grace Chiang, Founder of Cherish Parenting." LivingOS Newsletter. LivingOS, October 15, 2020.
https://livingos.substack.com/p/talk-show-spotlight-grace-chiang.

CHAPTER FIVE: BE YOURSELF

Allen-Ebrahimian, Bethany. "The Number of Chinese Students at US Universities Has Nearly Tripled over the Past Decade." *Axios*, April 29, 2020. https://www.axios.com/chinese-students-american-universities-d28c0ac2-5f65-435d-a8a2-efc8e7064e69.html.

Bao, Joyce and Charlene Wang. "Charlene Wang, Permission to Become a Model Breaker." December 16, 2020. In *Permission to Become*. Produced by Joyce Bao. Podcast. 43:49. https://anchor.fm/permissiontobecome/episodes/Ep-1---Charlene-Wang--Permission-to-Become-a-Model-Breaker-entjj9/a-a458q82.

Hong. *Minor Feelings*. Kindle.

Jost, John T. "A Theory of System Justification." American Psychological Association, June 2017. https://www.apa.org/science/about/psa/2017/06/system-justification.

Montlake, Simon. "For Chinese High-Schoolers, There's Value to Living and Learning in Iowa." The Christian Science Monitor. The Christian Science Monitor, October 4, 2018. https://www.csmonitor.com/EqualEd/2018/1004/For-Chinese-high-schoolers-there-s-value-to-living-and-learning-in-Iowa.

Pollock, D.C., and R.E. Van Reken. *Third Culture Kids: Growing Up Among Worlds*. Boston: Nicholas Brealy, 1999.

Wang, Charlene. "Issue #95 - LivingOS 2020 Year in Review." LivingOS.org, December 26, 2020. https://livingos.substack.com/p/-issue-95-livingos-2020-year-in-review.

CHAPTER SIX: TELL YOUR OWN STORY

Big Hit Labels. "BTS (방탄소년단) 'DNA' Official MV." September 18, 2017. Video, 4:15. https://youtu.be/MBdVXkSdhwU.

Big Hit Labels. "BTS (방탄소년단) '작은 것들을 위한 시 (Boy With Luv) (feat. Halsey)' Official MV." April 12, 2019. Video, 4:12. https://youtu.be/XsX3ATc3FbA.

Brown, Brené. *Rising Strong: How the Ability to Reset Transforms the Way We Live, Love, Parent, and Lead*. New York: Random House, 2017. Kindle.

CAPE (Coalition of Asian Pacifics in Entertainment). "#IAm Constance Wu Story." May 7, 2015. Video, 11:54. https://youtu.be/G4eNDPImQmw.

CAPE (Coalition of Asian Pacifics in Entertainment). "#IAm Sandra Oh Story." May 18, 2018. Video, 6:30. https://youtu.be/vgdLZbzES2w.

Constance Wu, Henry Golding, Michelle Yeoh, and Gemma Chan. *Crazy Rich Asians*. Directed by Chu, Jon M. Burbank, CA: Warner Bros. Pictures, 2018.

Matsumoto, Jon. "How K-Pop's US Popularity Is Exploding." GRAMMY.com. Recording Academy, August 27, 2020. https://www.grammy.com/grammys/news/why-k-pops-popularity-exploding-united-states.

Moore, Jacob. "K-Pop Takes Over Madison Square Garden." Complex, April 20, 2020. https://www.complex.com/music/2011/10/k-pop-takes-over-madison-square-garden.

officialpsy. "PSY - GANGNAM STYLE(강남스타일) M/V." July 15, 2012. Video, 4:12. https://youtu.be/9bZkp7q19f0.

Trust, Gary. "BTS' 'Dynamite' Adds to Record Run Atop Billboard's Global Charts." Billboard, January 11, 2021. https://www.billboard.com/articles/business/chart-beat/9509380/bts-dynamite-record-run-billboard-global-charts.

Wang, Lulu. *The Farewell.* United States: A24, 2019.

Wilkinson, Bard. "K-Pop Band BTS Tells World Youth to 'Speak Yourself' at UN." *Cable News Network*, September 25, 2018. https://www.cnn.com/2018/09/24/asia/bts-un-korea-intl/index.html.

CHAPTER SEVEN: TAKE RISKS

Doyle, Glennon. *Untamed.* New York: Dial Press, March 10, 2020.

CHAPTER EIGHT: BEING OKAY WITH NOT BEING OKAY

"Asian American/Pacific Islander Communities and Mental Health." Mental Health America. Accessed January 19, 2021. https://www.mhanational.org/issues/asian-americanpacific-islander-communities-and-mental-health.

Chen, Stacy. "Asian-American Women Want to End the Stigma around Mental Health Treatment." Good Morning America, September 10, 2018. https://www.goodmorningamerica.com/wellness/story/generation-asian-american-women-fighting-normalize-mental-health-57651825.

Karas. *Ali Wong: Baby Cobra.*

Karas. *Ali Wong: Hard Knock Wife.*

"Preventing Child Abuse & Neglect." Centers for Disease Control and Prevention. Centers for Disease Control and Prevention, April 7, 2020. https://www.cdc.gov/violenceprevention/childabuseandneglect/fastfact.html.

"Preventing Youth Violence." Centers for Disease Control and Prevention. Centers for Disease Control and Prevention, April 7, 2020. https://www.cdc.gov/violenceprevention/youthviolence/fastfact.html.

RSA. "Brené Brown on Empathy." December 10, 2013. Video, 2:53. https://youtu.be/1Evwgu369Jw.

Wiseman, Theresa. "A concept analysis of empathy." Journal of advanced nursing 23.6 (1996): 1162-1167.

CHAPTER NINE: TO THE NEXT GENERATION

Mental Health America, "Asian American/Pacific Islander Communities and Mental Health."

CHAPTER TEN: YOUNG PROFESSIONALS

"2019 Annual Intel Diversity and Inclusion Report." Intel, 2019. https://www.intel.com/content/www/us/en/diversity/diversity-inclusion-annual-report.html.

Guo, Jeff. "The Real Reasons the US Became Less Racist toward Asian Americans." *The Washington Post*, April 29, 2019. https://www.washingtonpost.com/news/wonk/wp/2016/11/29/the-real-reason-americans-stopped-spitting-on-asian-americans-and-started-praising-them/.

Staff, NPR. "Yul Kwon, From Bullying Target to Reality TV Star." *NPR*, May 15, 2012. https://www.npr.org/2012/05/16/152775069/yul-kwon-from-bullying-target-to-reality-tv-star.

Kraus, M. W., & Mendes, W. B. (2014). Sartorial symbols of social class elicit class-consistent behavioral and physiological responses: A dyadic approach. *Journal of Experimental Psychology: General, 143*(6), 2330–2340. https://doi.org/10.1037/xge0000023.

Kanze, Dana, Laura Huang, Mark A. Conley, and E. Tory Higgins. "Male and Female Entrepreneurs Get Asked Different Questions by VCs — and It Affects How Much Funding They Get." *Harvard Business Review*, June 27, 2017. https://hbr.org/2017/06/male-and-female-entrepreneurs-get-asked-different-questions-by-vcs-and-it-affects-how-much-funding-they-get.

Buck Gee and Denise Peck, "Asian Americans Are the Least Likely Group in the US to Be Promoted to Management," *Harvard Business Review*, May 31, 2018.

CHAPTER ELEVEN: CONCLUSION

Wang, Charlene. "Dear Warren." LivingOS.org, May 14, 2020. https://www.livingos.org/blog/dear-warren.

CPSIA information can be obtained
at www.ICGtesting.com
Printed in the USA
FSHW020623280421

9 781636 769561